dreamthink

By

D.C. Taylor

TABLE OF CONTENTS

DEDICATION

This book is dedicated to those who have hung by me throughout these many years. Through the good times and bad, through the wild times and not-so-wild times, and especially through those times when I wasn't there for you but I know that you were always there for me. Much love. Big ups to: Carolyn Taylor, Edward Taylor, Kathy Taylor, Mark Taylor, Matthew Taylor, Natalie Taylor, Robert Jackson, Jr., Merrill and Regina Owens, Kevin Hicks, Houston (Butch) Robinson, Jim Shipley, Stan Keitt, Chris Fielder, Michael Krauss, Karen Levy, Mike Bearden, Missy Leon, Cressida Biaton, Pam Tarr, Dale Szylodwski, Chris Hellems, Duane Turner, Nancy and Patti McGraw, Abby Kohler, Mr. and Mrs. Levy, Doug Winton, Jim McDonald, Gayle Route, Maurice Marable, Ed Pryor, Lawson and JoAnne Fisher, Paz (Tony) Villanova (for the title graphics), Lilliam Monroig, Mr. Mitchell, Joel Hinman, Peter Askin, David Shakes, Steve Julty, James Pride, Chris Nakis, Steve Boyne, Valerie Johnson, Sonya Wells, Arthur Herr (Mr. Mr.), Leonard Jones, Lisa Leone, Rodney Stringfellow, Phil Maillard, Paulette Clark, Kervin Simms, Janet McGill, Dr. Walter Cooper, Electa Brown, Mr. Bob Sagan, Arnold Kornbulth, Ruby and the many friends and acquaintances who changed my life.

And for those of you who aren't with us in this plane of reality, I look forward to seeing you in the next world: Marion and Dobbie Hicks, Edward Taylor, Jr., Mark Adams, Clark F.

Grain, Bill Tyus, Mrs. Jacobs, Mr. Hicks, Paul Williams, Uncle Hank, Mr. Sipple, Donald Johnson and Tobey Robinson. Thank you for making my life better.

I'd also like to thank the people whom I don't know but who have deeply influenced me and given me years of enjoyment: Alexandre Dumas, H.G. Wells, Jules Verne, Oscar Micheaux, Douglas Adams, Steven King, Dean Koontz, John Grisham, Tom Clancy, Ralph Bakshi, all Three Stooges (even Shemp, and especially Curly), Monty Python, Rod Serling, Brian Benben, the Kids in the Hall, John Frankenheimer, Quentin Tarantino, Robert Rodriguez, Ray Harryhousen, Clive Cussler, Charlie Chaplin, Steven Donaldson, Walt Disney, Albert Einstein, Peter Askin, Peter Newman, Penn and Teller, Larry Miller, Steve Martin, George Carlin, Harry Houdini, David Blaine, Octavia Butler, Robin Williams, Walter Mosley, Richard Matheson, James Patterson, Jon Deever, *Laugh-In*, Steven Spielberg, George Lucas, M. Night Shyamalan, Sid Caesar, Woody Allen, Mel Brooks, Al Brooks, Clarence Williams III, the Cohen brothers, Alfred Hitchcock, Robert Zemeckis, Oliver Stone, the Tina and Louise Restaurant, Richard Pryor, Steve Harvey, Cedric the Entertainer, Robin Williams, Jonathan Winters, Bill Gates, Colombo, Banachek, *Star Trek* (all the series; give *Enterprise* a chance), Red Dwarf, *Dr Who*, *The Prisoner*, *The Avengers*, *The Night Stalker*, *The King of Queens*, *Seinfeld*, *Wings*, *Just Shoot Me*, *The X-Files*, Mary Tyler Moore, Bob Newhart, the cast of *It's a Mad, Mad, Mad, Mad World* (which ought to be remade), D.F. Jones, the Rat

Pack, *The Outer Limits, Dream On, The Larry Sanders Show*, Marvel and DC comics, Frank Miller, Staples, Radio Shack, *The Wiz*, The Sci-fi Channel, The Comedy Channel, The History Channel, The Food Channel (I love to cook, ask anyone), HBO, Cinemax, Showtime, and every video store that I used to belong to (you know who you are). I would like to thank all the above for giving me great pleasure while I wasn't writing, allowing me to recharge my creative and emotional batteries.

AUTHOR'S NOTE

Dream Think is a concept that has been with humankind since the beginning of time. Many cultures, ranging from Native American to Asian to African, have used it to survive for generations. Dream Thinking (i.e., daydreaming) is defined in *Webster's New World Dictionary* as: 1. A pleasant feeling and filled with a series of thoughts. 2. A visionary scheme.

Dream Thinking is something everyone does. It frees us from everyday hardships and misfortunes. Some of our best and brightest ideas have come from staring off into space, letting the mind roam to search other dimensions and ideas. I'm certain that Bach, Einstein, Gates, Dumas and many others made their greatest discoveries while Dream Thinking. No matter who comes up with the next great idea, is likely that Dream Thinking will be responsible.

This book presents a series of daydreams that I have had through the years. I turned these thoughts into short stories, short film scripts and film treatments. As you can tell by the dates in the table of contents, these stories were written throughout my career. I figured that I had to start somewhere. Some are better than others, but all emerged from Dream Thinking.

Before each story I describe what I was doing at the time these stories came to me. I figure that my mindset at the time is as important as the story itself

So sit back in your favorite chair and read these ideas with an open mind. Believe me, you will need one.

'Nuff said, let's git wit it ...

INTRODUCTION

"Life is what happens while you're busy making other plans"
—Unknown

Growing up in the suburbs of Rochester, NY, I lived for one thing and one thing only: television. I couldn't wait to get home to watch whatever was on. I'd watch anything. My friends would come over on a Saturday morning to play and all I wanted to do was watch. Like most parents, my folks put a curfew on watching TV on a school night. This just meant I watched more on the weekends. The thing that fascinated me about it was the places it took me. The Three Stooges made me laugh to no end. Gregory the Gravewalker, the local Saturday night scary-movie guy, walked through a cemetery introducing often bad but nonetheless scary films. He often scared me more than the movies themselves. *Star Trek* allowed me to travel to the outer reaches of the known and unknown universe. *The Twilight Zone* opened up the possibilities of other realities.

I can remember the first movie that made me cry like it was yesterday. It was *The Red Balloon*, on *The Kukla, Fran and Ollie* show. Even through the film was German-made, the images and music that got to me. I was eight years old.

My mom sometimes tells stories of my early television days. There is one of me hiding behind a big chair in the living room while *Night Gallery* aired. The one that really got me was the one with Ozzie Davis playing the butler who drove his boss, Roddy McDowell, mad by changing the pictures in his house. Man, I still get a shiver just thinking about it. (The Wicked Witch of the West did a number on me too. Teaming her up with those damn flying monkeys gave me nightmares for weeks.) The other has to do with me crying my eyes out as Maria held a dying Tony in her arms in *West Side Story*. Okay, I admit it: I was easily affected by the things I saw and heard. (I defy anyone to admit that they didn't drop a tear during Billy Dee's deathbed scene in *Brian's Song*. James Caan's reaction alone would bring anyone to his or her emotional knees. Come on people, have a heart.)

I always remember our house being filled with music. Classical, choral, jazz, funk, rock and pop played throughout the house. The entire spectrum was heard. My father was a music teacher who gave voice and piano lessons from the house. My brother took piano lessons for many years, and my mom and sister could knock out a pretty good tune on the ivories too. I tried the drums and violin but they didn't take. I did have an okay voice until it changed (some people say it still hasn't). Both my parents made sure that their kids had a well-rounded education in the arts. I remember attending concerts, plays, museums, the circus and the Ice Capades year after year. The thing that I truly loved about all these events was the exposure to new things and experiences. They seemed to open my mind, freeing it ...

Okay, hold up a second. I have to stop this heartrending

rollercoaster for a moment and straighten something out. Right about now you might be thinking: "Why the hell is he telling me all this shit? So he had a good home life. Damn, I watched television too; that's no big deal. What's the rumpus?"

Okay you might not use the word *rumpus*, but I like it (see *Miller's Crossing* by the Cohen brothers). I have to admit that I found the Ice Capades a little boring. Sorry, Mom, but it's the truth.

I guess what I'm trying to say is that being exposed to all these things allowed me to see that there was a much larger world out there to explore. I found that the best way to explore this new world was through television, movies and books. My folks were always taking us to the movies. There is something about sitting in a darkened theater watching larger-than-life images that gets to you. I remember my uncle Hank taking my sister and me to see *The Swiss Family Robinson* or going to see *Alien* with my father and brother. *Slap Shot, Star Wars, Saturday Night Fever, Uptown Saturday Night, Let's Do It Again* and any Bruce Lee movie (take your pick: *Enter the Dragon* and *Return of the Dragon* are the best) filled my head with images and sounds that I remember to this day.

As I got older I became more active in sports (football, baseball, basketball and soccer), both in school and during the summer. I would imagine myself hitting the winning home run or scoring the winning goals, just like my heroes in the movies. Sometimes this would happen, but more often it didn't. (See *Rollerball, The Natural, Blood of Heroes, Kingpin, Major*

League, etc.)

School was something that I had to do. It was my job. Both my folks worked very hard to give their family what they needed. I have this theory that only 3 percent of society is really doing what they love and making a living at it. This is something that my parents both taught me: never settle; never surrender.

During my youth I remember getting my friends together and putting on impromptu performances of *Oliver* and *Jesus Christ Superstar* for anyone who would come. Mostly they were my mom's friends, who were just being polite. We went all out: music, cheap sets, even costumes. I can remember during one performance getting temperamental and walking off because our audience wasn't taking us seriously. I want to take this time to apologize to the following people: Kathy Taylor (my sister), Pam Tarr, Patty and Nancy McGraw, Abby Kohler, Chris Hellems and anyone else I embarrassed. I know what you're thinking: "We have a thespian on our hands!" I just liked producing and directing shows, that's it ... end of story.

After high school, I attended Howard University. My first year was a nightmare. I missed my friends and my old life. It wasn't until my second year that I hit my stride. I got involved in activities that opened my mind and spirit. The other thing was that people started to listen to my ideas for the first time. This was the first time I can remember Dream Thinking. I put some of these ideas into my early scriptwriting class work and other outside work.

I hated writing in high school and college, and in fact I had to take freshman English twice in order to pass. However, when I was allowed to create something without the constraints of rules, my thoughts became clear.

One of the first memories I have of living in Brooklyn was riding home on the D train at five a.m. after working at ABC Television. I had fallen asleep on the train (yes, it was stupid), and awoke to find my wallet gone. I asked the guy next to me if he had seen anything. He laughed and told me that I shouldn't have fallen asleep on the train. I was pissed. When we arrived at the DeKalb station a white couple jumped up and told me and the guy sitting next to me to get off the train. They told me that they were off-duty undercover cops out on a date. They threw me the guy's bag. My wallet was inside. He started to yell that he was just out of jail and didn't want to go back. He told me to hit him to make it even. I did ... and then told the cops to take him off to jail.

I can remember the thing that really made me start to write. I was at home watching *Entertainment Tonight* when Richard Pryor came on to announce the formation of his new production company, Indigo Films with Jim Brown (unfortunately they only made one film, *Jo Jo Dancer, Your Life Is Calling*). A reporter asked Pryor where his script ideas would come from. He turned to the camera and said, "Our ideas could come from someone who is watching on television right now."

I could have sworn he was talking right to me. That's when I started to write my first feature-film script. I wrote it by hand on a legal pad. It was about two kids who decide to try and save the Apollo Theater. Some shady real-estate developers are planning to buy it, tear it down and turn it into condos. The kids hold a fundraiser, bringing back many of the stars that had performed there over the years. I wanted Eddie Murphy and Michael Jackson to star in it. I still have the script in a drawer somewhere ...

I want to grind to a halt again to talk about something. I know a lot of people will think that this is total bullshit (because some of my friends have told me so), but where and when they did their best work is important. You basically find out they write from five a.m. to about nine a.m., then pick it up again late in the evening for about three hours. This is precisely the schedule I keep. In between I reread what I penned, and make notes. I try and take a total break and do everyday things like the rest of society. If I'm writing a script I can knock out five to seven pages per day (ten on a good day). Now you're thinking: "Hold on there, son! Seven to ten pages ... that means you could finish a script in two weeks!" Yes I could, but it doesn't mean it would be any good. The way it breaks down is basically one page of script equals one minute on the screen. Now, you could write a line that says "car chase." This event could last fifteen minutes.

When a script is written, one element always presents itself. It may have a lot of characters or special effects or a lot of locations. These elements will determine the difficulty of making it happen. Three things will always be the key to getting it done: time, money and quality. If you don't have a lot of time but you have a lot of money you get quality. If you don't have a lot of time *or* money you get low quality. That's how it works.

The other thing is where you write. Here's what works for me: In the morning I like to write on my desktop in my office (OK … it's a corner in my apartment, but it's nice). In the afternoon I'll get out and make my notes in a totally different place. I get this tunnel-vision thing when I'm working, and before I know it I'm immersed in the story. I also have a laptop, which allows me to move around the apartment and to outside areas to change up my writing environment. Like I said, it works for me.

Like most writers, I have been asked by several people where my ideas come from. Years ago I came up with an exercise that helps me think. It's very simple. I just ask myself the "What if ?" question. I know that I'm not the first person to think of this technique. I do know that it works for me. For example, I asked myself: "What if the boogie man was real?" or "What if the Four Horsemen of the Apocalypse came to earth to do their thing and one of them got lost on the way here. How would it play out?" It's a game I play. Sometimes nothing comes of it, but other times it sparks an idea … a dream … a Dream Thought.

One of the other things that always continue to fascinate me is the written or spoken word. I know I'm stating the obvious (I'm a writer, after all), but I collect them as a hobby. It is usually based on something that I have heard or read. Sometimes they're just single words like *juxtaposition, cornucopia* or *rumpus*. Sometimes they're groupings of words like: "If things go right we'll all be sitting in butter." (*Wings*); "Rack and pinion steering, get out of here you half a sissy before I give you a slap." (*Easy Money*); "When I want your opinion I'll beat it out of you." (Chuck Norris); "Say whose kung fu is the best, say it." (*The X-Files*); "What's the rumpus?" (*Miller's Crossing*) or "It's just two tears in a bucket, fuck it ... let's take it to the stage." (George Clinton). I can't really explain why I like these combinations of words or phrases; they just sound cool to me.

One of the hardest things to write is dialogue in stories or in scripts. I have been told that I have the knack. I question this because it is hard to write how people speak. What I do as an exercise is listen to people. Everyone has a distinct voice. It isn't always about an accent or education. The way people talk is how they express themselves. Some use their hands, while others speak softly. It's true that people say more when they are silent than when they speak. It's not always about what people say; it's more about when or how they say it. A lot of actors who direct or write have their characters saying these long monologues that they think are deep. This is not always the best way to go. What I try to do is let my characters find their voices. I have an exercise that helps me do this: I put each new character I am developing into a mugging situation. I ask myself, "How would this person act if he or she were mugged?" Would they run or talk their way out of it? Maybe they would fight or give up their wallet willingly. Personally, I would give up my wallet without thinking about it. I can always make more money or get new credit cards. It's just two tears in a bucket ...

I guess what I'm trying to say is that there are techniques that help me develop my stories and characters. They may not work for you but I thought I'd throw them in here. Hell, they may not work for me either. Like I said before, this is my first attempt at a book.

I'll be the first to say that it's not always as simple as using the exercises I listed above. Over the years I've discovered that I'm what I call a jag or frenzy writer. Months will go by where nothing new comes. Then *bam!*—I write like crazy for three months. The down time is spent rewriting, and developing old ideas. I read books, scripts and watch movies. It helps me to recharge.

So give these stories a chance and see what happens. Who knows, you may start to Dream Think yourself...

Chapter 1

I2
(INNOCENT INTELLIGENCE)

"Communication is the problem to the answer."
—Jade'

INTRODUCTION

I had been laid off by the American Broadcasting Company (ABC) in the winter of 1983 and found work through a friend, Clark F. Grain. I had gone to Howard University with Clark, and we'd stayed in touch through the years. When I was out of work I called him and we talked. He told me that the Satellite News Channel (SNC) was looking for people. I called and got an interview, and later on a job. The work wasn't hard and I met some people who helped me develop my writing talents. One of those people was Jim McDonald, one of the funniest people I have ever met.

While at SNC I made inroads to developing a series of minute-long episodes about sporting legends called *The Greatest*. The first one explored the world of Dr. J. I left this job to return to ABC, but returned when I was laid off again. By that time SNC had been bought by Ted Turner, who closed down the facility before the ink was dry on the check. By 1985 it was renting its services out to independent productions. The first one that bit was Michael Krauss Productions. He was then married to Joan Lunden and was producing something called *Mothers' Minutes*. I was hired as a freelance Chryon operator. It was an easy job, which allowed me a lot of time to write.

One day they had a baby expert on discussing the intelligence of babies. He said that science really didn't know how intelligent babies were. It was something that we may never know. This information stuck with me. I began to develop a story based on this idea. I remember going home to the "Roch" for a visit. It was there that the idea came into focus for me. I remember writing it at the foot of my parents' bed while watching a new channel called HBO.

After writing this story I wrote a lot of shorts with Jim, and became friends with Michael Krauss. I had heard that *Saturday Night Live* was looking for writers for their new season. I had made contact with them. They told me that they were only accepting writers represented by agents. When I told Michael, he called his agent at William Morris and got Jim and me an interview. It was two weeks away, so we had time to write more skits and ideas. Well, let me just say that I never wrote for *SNL* and I am not signed with William Morris. My mom says life is what happens in between your plans. This is proof positive. But out of this experience I came up with my first collection of skits and stories.

It was worth it.

After writing this story, I gave it to a friend who was working as a receptionist at *Omni* magazine. They were publishing some great stories that I loved and I wanted to get my story in there. I heard nothing from them. In 1999, a movie was released entitled *Super Geniuses*, starring Kathleen Turner. It was almost an exact duplicate of my story. I was pissed, so I called my attorney and told him about it. He asked me if I had copyrighted it and I told him I hadn't. There was nothing I could do about it. I learned a lesson that day that will live with me forever: COPYRIGHT EVERYTHING!

12

(INNOCENT INTELLIGENCE)

Joe looks over his completed manifesto with a sense of accomplishment. He can feel in his bones that his time is getting closer. He knows that his mind will begin to slowly slip away, leaving him nothing more than a vegetable. The clock is slowly but steadily ticking away the last moments of his present existence. The only thing he has left to do is look over the document, and then all will be ready. He takes a long, deep breath and focuses all of his mental facilities on the crudely written paper that lies before him. It is unfortunate that he had to write his thesis in crayon, but that is all he had at his disposal. Knowing time is short, he decides just to hit the high points. He begins to read.

CHAPTER I

My entrance into this world was filled with fear, terror and, believe it or not, violence. I felt something grabbing at my legs and pulling me out of the dark, warm, wet place I had called home for as long as I could remember. There was a blinding flash of light, a whack on my hindquarters and a rush of cold air all over my naked body. The next thing I remembered doing was crying my fucking eyes out. That shit hurt. I slowly opened my eyes to see a bunch of giants looking at me, passing me back and forth like a rubber ball. Well, my crying seemed to make the big uns (this is what I named the giant animal-like species) happy for some strange reason. Talk about some weird behavioral traits (see behavioral study in Chapter IV). I suddenly felt extremely tired. I closed my eyes and went to sleep.

I opened my eyes to find that I was in a large glass room together with many of my brothers and sisters. I looked up through the glass partition and saw a bunch of the big uns staring at us and—get this—making inane faces. I knew right then and there that their size had nothing to do with their level of intelligence. I was dealing with mental midgets. In the sea of faces I recognized one male big un who was waving like a man possessed. I thought I'd give him a thrill and wave back at him for kicks. He was so excited I thought he would have a brain aneurysm. I suddenly felt exhausted again and drifted off to sleep. On the verge of going to sleep I could faintly feel the telepathic power of my mind growing with every breath I took into my small lungs.

...

Joe looks up from his manuscript and rubs his tired eyes. From the beginning, Joe had known that there was more to being a baby than having a warm place to sleep and eat every day. He had been right in this assessment but it has taken a while for him to prove his theory. He notices that his breathing has quickened for some reason. He checks his pulse. His heart is racing. Sweat drips into his eyes, making them burn and tear from the salt. He wipes the sweat and pain away and focuses on a replica of a species of animal called a teddy bear. He looks into its button eyes, concentrating on maintaining control for a while longer. It takes all of his mental energy to get his bodily functions to a normal rate. He knows his time is getting close. He picks up his manuscript, quickly flips some pages and continues reading.

CHAPTER III

I awoke with a start, and realized I was sucking on something soft and warm. It was attached to the female of the big un species. A warm, wet, sweet substance emerged from the soft mound of flesh. As I sucked, I felt that my telepathic power had grown in strength. I tried to scan the female's mind and found that there was nothing to read. But I saw something I didn't quite understand. It didn't scare me, but it was a feeling I couldn't decipher. All that concerned me was that they continued to take care of me. Since they couldn't communicate with me, maybe I was misreading their intentions.

It was then that I theorized that their brainpower index did not expend the energy level needed to communicate with a higher intelligence like myself. I fell asleep with this thought on my mind.

CHAPTER V

Over the next couple of months I decided to learn as much as I could about the big uns in their own environment. I was fascinated with what I called their Primitive Brain Power Index

(PBPI). (Please see psychological behavioral maze studies on PBPI in Chapter XI.) It struck me as a horrible existence. The lack of communication caused me to yearn for some kind of mental stimulation.

It took about eight months, in the big uns' time line, until I had direct visual contact with other beings like myself. Up until this time I had limited long-distance telepathic contact with other minds. It wasn't so much contact, but a gentle nudging that seemed to exercise, THERE WAS no strengthening of my intellect. Unfortunately, that contact was very short and faint. It was like someone or something was testing me.

On October 13, 1985, I was taken to a building with many beings like myself in it. Up until that point, my world had consisted of basically one room. I had no idea that there was such a wondrous world outside. The sights and sounds were at first overwhelming to my senses, but I gained control after several minutes had passed.

The first thought that entered my mind was: "How could a race of beings that put out such a PBPI build such a vast and beautiful world?"

Well, this question and many others would be answered for me. My life was about to change in ways I couldn't imagine on my best day.

When I entered the building, my mind was bombarded by thoughts that were not my own. My mind hurt so much I thought it would explode from the pressure. All I could do to fight it was cry my eyes out. The female big un that was carrying me put me down and left the room. I looked around and saw that the room was filled with beings like me. It was a strange, yet calming feeling. Several of them crawled over to me. At first, all I heard in my mind was extremely fast-sounding gibberish. One of them came over to me and stroked my head, relaxing me. Soon the sounds slowed to a point where I could understand them. He told me that his name was Anubis, and told me not to worry because I was among friends. I finally felt my mind relax and decided to go with the flow; besides, the mental stimulation felt fantastic. Before I could even ask a question, Anubis had an answer for me: "This place is called 'HERE.' Each place that you resided in other than this place is called 'THERE.' The elders of BABYHOOD have decided to keep things simple."

"Who are—" I began, but he interrupted.

"The elders of BABYHOOD are those I2's (Innocent Intelligences) with the ability to communicate with other I2s telepathically in other 'HERES.' There was an elder in each 'HERE.' In each 'THERE' that particular I2 was the elder."

Anubis continued to explain that when I was in my "THERE" the thoughts that I was hearing were the elders trying to exercise my telepathic power index.

I thought: "I2s?"

He thought: "Our intelligence in relation to the big uns' world has yet to be recognized or 'born.' Therefore, our intelligence is untainted or influenced by the powers that be. In more basic terms, we are innocent."

It was decided that our sole purpose in life was to try to establish a communication link between the big uns and us.

Many things were tried through the centuries, but they had all failed. In the beginning it was noticed that the big uns seemed to be oblivious to the fact that our intelligence even existed. The very fact that we were born with all knowledge meant that we had a lot to give their world. The end of hunger, disease and poverty would just be the beginning. The first I2 born in this reality, Jade', knew from her first thought that something had to be done. She set up our Standard Operating Procedure (SOP), which has not changed since day one. All of what we know is based on her teachings. It was she who foresaw the coming of one that would show us the way. It wasn't until the third phase of our empire that the Senility Bridge was discovered. This is the boundary that represents the distance in the communication levels between the big uns and us.

Jade' described it as: "Communication is the problem to the answer."

I asked him if anyone had ever crossed this bridge and maintained contact.

"No," he answered.

They had tried several manned missions, as well as group exploration, but nothing worked. It was said that one would be born who would show us the way with a simple thought. A chosen one who would lead both worlds into a new, enlightened age.

Through the eons the elders had documented the characteristics of traveling across the bridge:

A. Loss of I2 mental facilities

B. Loss of ability to communicate with other I2s

C. Toward the end, the I2's brain index is equal to the big uns.

D. It is believed that once the brain index is balanced out, communication with the big uns is established.

The next thing he told me knocked my socks off. Everyone in BABYHOOD eventually crosses the Senility Bridge. Everyone. It seems that when an I2 reaches an age of twelve to fourteen months, he or she goes through the transformation. This seems to be related to an I2 beginning to speak his or her first words in the big uns' language. All we know is that the process is irreversible. I got upset and scared when I realized that I would lose my newfound telepathic power and become like the slow-witted big uns. It was then that the elders revealed to me that they tried to prepare each I2 for the experience.

"Prepare how?" I inquired.

"The process is designed to give that I2 what they will need to handle the journey," an elder with a Japanese thought accent answered.

"When will I be prepared?" I asked.

"In due time.... In due time..." They answered together.

It was then that I understood why the sole purpose of the I2's was to successfully cross the Senility Bridge.

...

Joe looks up from his manuscript when he hears the female big un enter the room. Over time, he came to know her as "Ma" and the male as "Da." As he gets closer to his time, he starts to understand some of the simple speech patterns of the big uns' communication. He wonders what it would be like over on the other side. Joe gazes into her eyes as she picks him up and cuddles him in her arms.

When he first started writing his thesis, Joe wondered if the big uns could comprehend what he was writing. On occasion one of them would look at his paper and put it down unread. He came up with a theory that the farther one got from the transformation stage in time, the ability to communicate at all with anyone or anything to do with BABYHOOD decreased. He turns back to his crudely written document.

CHAPTER VII

The past several weeks have been nothing short of mind blowing. I took the position of second elder in my "HERE." The changing of the guard in BABYHOOD was a frequent occurrence due to the fact that the elders were constantly going across the bridge. Anubis taught me many things about the big uns and I2s. The most important item is that we, the big uns and the I2s, are the same species. The big uns have all the knowledge and intelligence we have, but for some reason, as yet unknown, going over the bridge places limitations on the mind. Some have theorized that fear and self doubt obstruct them from achieving their true potential. The thing that makes us intelligent is our total belief that all is possible and nothing is impossible. This fact is enlightening to say the least.

...

Joe falls asleep from exhaustion for a minute, but awakes with a start. He flips some pages and continues on.

CHAPTER X

Believing that everything is possible, I decided to find a way across the Senility Bridge that separates our two worlds. The first thing I noticed was that everything in BABYHOOD was of an oral nature. What I mean is that nothing was written down or recorded on anything. Our brains have the ability to learn and retain anything we see or hear. This small but important detail gave me the basis for my theory. One day, while hanging out with Anubis, I held up a piece of paper with some writing on it. He read it and looked at me.

"You know that we don't have to write anything down. We're I2's ..." he said.

I told him that my hypothesis consisted of writing down all the facts of BABYHOOD and crossing the bridge. All that a person would have to do was read it as soon as he crossed over. Simple but sweet. Anubis sat for a moment and then put out such a telepathic mind blast that it physically knocked me over. Soon after that the air was filled with the thoughts of all the elders of all the "HERES" from the four corners of the earth. They thought so fast and loud that I tried to clear my mind of their thoughts. Then, as soon as it had started, it stopped. The air was still once again. Anubis turned to me and opened his eyes. He smiled and told me that it had been decided. I was the one that the I2s had been waiting for. I was the chosen one who would go across the bridge with the document and bring our two worlds together.

The next several months were spent planning how the

manuscript should be formatted and written. It was decided that it should be written in a simple language so that the big uns could understand it. The main body of the text should center on an I2's life in BABYHOOD. To prove that what it says was the real thing, the elders decided to give them the genetic sequence for a formula that would rid the world of cancer. To establish a hard link between both worlds, the document would include the design for a device that would magnify the big uns' brainpower index to our level. Once a link had been established we would work together to make this world the utopia it could be. I took on my newfound responsibility with great fervor.

...

Joe stops reading when he realizes that he has just pissed on himself. He has been doing that more and more lately. He starts to cry to get the big uns' attention, but no one comes. He starts to worry but relaxes when he sees Ol' Ma enter the room. Joe thinks it is interesting that he feels more of a connection with the older big uns. They seem to take life at a more relaxed pace. In fact, he realizes that the older the big uns get, the closer they come to achieving actual communication with the I2's. It was once reported that an I2 elder established a brief connection with a 101-year-old female big un. However, the link was severed when the I2 crossed over and the big un expired. It is a vicious circle. After he is changed he turns his attention back to the document in question. Joe comes to a point in the manuscript that makes him shed a tear.

CHAPTER XII

One day, while discussing the dynamics of relationships among the I2s, Anubis stopped in mid-thought. I asked the question again, but didn't get a reply. I looked up at him and saw that he was just staring off into space. I asked him what was wrong. When he didn't answer, I knew that he had gone over. My thoughts picked up a faint cry: "It's him!"

I reached out to him with all my might and heard him think: "By all the elders ... it's not that baaaad... *aahh!*"

I reached over to touch my lost comrade, only to find a shell. I let out a scream of pain and frustration. My call was answered by several of the elders. They explained that he might not be one with us in this reality but he was not gone. I didn't understand. They told me that his essence had gone back to the beginning to start anew. Being that we are of a higher intelligence we have the ability at this stage not be dependent on our physical presence. This most likely changes once we go through the void. Knowing this made me relax a bit, and further understand that life is a circle that never ends.

I watched as he crawled away toward the closest big un and climbed into her arms. I cried, not for the loss of a friend but because I couldn't travel across with him.

One day, while riding in a metal cart in a large building filled with many food products, I saw her for the first time. She was in a cart like mine, and it was heading right for me. As usual, the big uns pushing the vehicles were not looking where they were going, and *pow!*—food products everywhere! It was at this moment that I made telepathic contact with her. This contact was different in some way. Nothing had ever felt like this before. My body tingled all over. She allowed me to enter her mind easily, and without resistance. It felt so nice that I closed my eyes to get the full impact of the stimulation. She quickly withdrew, leaving me alone with my thoughts. I opened my eyes to find that she was gone. The next several days were filled with a mad search for my lover. Even though I had the ability to reach out to every I2 in the world I could not locate her. I find my mind yearning for her thoughts. We had only spent a moment together but it seemed like an eternity. It felt as though our minds had been one forever.

After searching to no avail, I sat still and tried to remember the experience. The thoughts felt so real, so good. It was like it was happening all over again. I quickly turned to see her sitting across the room in my "HERE."

I crawled over to her and thought: "Why couldn't I find you?"

"I blocked you out to teach you a lesson," she told me.

"Why?" I thought.

"To teach you about love," she said.

"What's love got to do with it?" I thought.

She laughed. "Love is the one element that we want you take with you."

"Hold on a minute. I understand what love is ..." I answered.

"That's true. You comprehend what love is, but what you didn't know is how it feels in here." She reached over and touched my heart. "What you are about to do is the most important thing any being has ever done. You had to experience what love is so you could explain to the big uns that we are one and love them with no conditions," she explained.

I thought about that for a moment, and realized that expressing this feeling to the big uns was key to the success of my mission. I remembered how the big uns looked when they held me in their arms. I hadn't understood it then, but now it hit me. Even though they didn't know a thing about me they loved me. This would be the one thing that they would truly understand.

Our minds melded into one for one last fling. We both sat there in ecstasy, together again.

...

Joe lets out a long, sad sigh as he finishes reading his manuscript. He signs it with a flourish. A wave of dizziness overcomes him and he lies back to clear his head. The thoughts of all the elders tell him that his time has come and that he takes along with him the hopes of every I2 in this reality. Joe feels his mind start to slip away. He tries to fight it at first, but realizes that he cannot mess with fate. He relaxes and decides to go with the flow. He turns to see Ma and Da enter the room. Everything seems to slow down. All the light in room disappears and is replaced by a rainbow of colors. He feels a strong wind blow over him. He looks down and sees himself sitting on the floor with his big uns. All of a sudden there is a flash of white light and he is back in his body. He hears strange voices. However, they are not in his head. They are coming from the big uns. He looks closely at their mouths as they speak. After a few moments, he starts to understand them.

In complete awe, Joe hears Ma say: "What's this Joey has been playing with?"

Joe watches as his parents pick up the thesis he has so carefully put together.

"Hold it up in front of him and see what he does," Da says.

They put the document up to his face. Joe lets out a long, blood-curdling scream when he realizes that the document the he had so carefully written looks like baby scribble. He can't read it. As he slips across the void, he screams in horror.

Chapter 2
A Random Dream Thought ...

FROM AFAR ...

I loved her from the moment I first saw her ...

Now, I'm the type of person who doesn't say "I love you" until I truly feel it in a relationship. To date I have said it five times in my life. Those occasions were the real deal. What I mean is that I didn't say it right before climaxing (everyone is guilty of that, and if you say you aren't you're a liar); it was a well-thought-out thing.

Upon seeing her in all her beauty and splendor, all I wanted to do was scream it from the top of my lungs so that everyone could hear.

But I didn't. I kept it inside as a strangled scream dying to get out. You see, I was with my best friend, Greg, when we met her and her friends in the pub on the Howard campus. Greg and I had become instant best friends upon meeting each other on our first day at college. We were assigned to be roommates in the freshman dorm. After three years we became closer, relying on each other for things we lacked. He gave me confidence in myself and I in turn gave him the structure and organization that his life needed. It was a mutually beneficial relationship, and had worked for both of us until now. But seeing her changed everything.

My life would never be the same.

I told Greg that I liked her and that I wanted to send her a drink anonymously. He said: "I bet you won't." So I called the bartender over and did it.

My heart raced. I knew that this might be the connection that would affect my life forever. He delivered the Long Island iced tea and told her that it was from someone in the bar. I watched as she and her friends looked around searching for eye contact. I looked down. When I looked up I saw Greg lifting his glass to them. Before he left me he said that he would "chat me up," and gave me a wink and a smile. I watched as he sauntered over to my dream girl.

They sat together for a long time, talking and laughing. When they got up to leave I stood up, not knowing what to do. They walked right by me, stopping only for a brief introduction. I was tongue-tied, but managed to blurt out a shaky "Hello." They told me that they were headed to a sorority rush party and she could only bring one other person.

I sat back down and nursed my beer, thinking that once again I had gotten the shaft.

Later on he tried to explain that he was really trying to sell me to her, but I wasn't sure. Greg would always take the lead. I didn't mind; in fact, I liked being his backup. It was how our relationship worked.

But I loved her with all my heart and soul. Really, I did ...

Let's stop for a moment.

Have you ever seen someone you didn't know who you thought was the one? Everything about them was perfect. The looks, the attitude, everything. I remember seeing a girl on a ferry in Washington, D.C. on a visit. I fell in love right then and there. To this day I remember what she was wearing (a white cotton dress with a white hat, just like Glenn Close in *The Natural*).

The heart is a funny thing ... They say that you can't pick your family or who your neighbors are. Well, I would like to add another: You can't pick who you choose to fall in love with. The heart wants what the heart wants. Period.

No questions asked ... it is what it is. 'Nuff said.

Well, to continue on with the story, I watched through the years as my best friend and my girl fell deeper and deeper in love. We became the trio; the threesome that often happens to a lot of friends. Oh we would double date from time to time, but in a strange way I felt like I was cheating on her. I know that sounds stupid, but what can I say? There were times during our four years at college that I will keep in my heart to the day I die. On one occasion I remember she came to me in tears after a fight that she and Greg had. "It's over," she sobbed. I held her and told her that things would be all right in time. But before I could make my move, he called me to tell me about what happened. They spoke, made up and according to him had the best sex they had had to date. There's nothing like make-up sex.

After graduation, they announced that they were getting married. I was the best man. At the stag party, Greg pulled me aside and in tears asked me for my permission to marry his bride. I looked at him for a long time, thinking about what to say. Finally, I hugged him tightly and whispered, "Of course!" We both cried that night, and I stood next to him the next day as they became husband and wife.

Through the years we stayed in touch, meeting on holidays to celebrate the happy times.

They had been married five years when she called me up to say that Greg was ill with cancer. He had ignored it for years but he was losing a battle that he could not win. I went to them for support. On his deathbed, Greg called me over, saying he had a request.

"Take care of my family... Promise me ..."

In tears, I nodded.

Before he passed, he said one more thing: "It took some time, but I told you I'd make it work out ..." he said. And then he died in my arms.

The family came in. I stepped back, trying to hold my feelings at bay while the family grieved. She asked me what his last words were. I couldn't tell her.

She slapped me in face. To this day I will never forget the anger in her eyes.

For a long time I stayed away from them. I tried dating, but nothing took. I tried calling her several times but she would only hang up on me. I'm not the stalking type, but I would find myself driving by her house trying to catch a glimpse of her. How sad is that?

On every anniversary of Greg's death I would go to the cemetery to talk to my friend. I would go early and watch as she and her family visited her dead husband. Only when they left would I go in and speak to my friend.

The years went by. I became very successful as a screenwriter in Hollywood. I kept an apartment in Washington, D.C., to get out of the business that is called show.

One day in D.C., I went to an Appleby's looking for a drink and trying to clear my head. That's when I heard a voice I hadn't heard in years. I looked up and saw her with some friends. I called the bartender over and ordered a drink for her: a Long Island iced tea. She asked who sent it, and he pointed over to me. I lifted my glass. She smiled, realizing for the first time that I was the one who had sent the first one so many years ago.

She slowly came over and we talked as if for the first time.

... And we lived happily ever after. Yeah, right ... but that's another tale.

Chapter 3

BOOGIE

"Monster, monster go away ... Monster, monster stay away."
—Big Guy

INTRODUCTION

The origin of this story is probably the strangest of all the tales in this book. I swear to God that it really happened. It definitely adds credence to the saying that truth is stranger than fiction.

It was the fall of 1988. I was employed as a tape editor at ABC. It was a slow evening, and I was returning from lunch with several friends. We had just finished busting our asses editing some show that afternoon, so I was looking forward to a nice, easy evening of hanging out with my buddies. I was walking past one of the many post-production editing suites when I heard the phone ring. This was odd in itself, because the room was empty and dark. This would most likely mean that it was a wrong number dialed by one of the many producers, production assistants or interns looking for someone who was long gone. I waited for several moments, but it went on ringing so I picked it up. On the other end I heard the scared voice of a small boy. All he said was, "Is my mommy there?" At first I thought it was one of my friends fucking around. I had images of me turning around and seeing them calling me from another phone, laughing their asses off. When I looked around I saw that I was alone. The place was a ghost town. Tumbleweeds and everything. When my mind cleared, I thought that maybe it was kids messing around. I could see them sitting at home, smoking dope, trying to muffle their drug-induced giggling. The thing that changed my mind was something that I heard in the child's voice. What I heard was terror. This was a child alone. I flashed back to my own childhood, when I had come home one day to find no one home but the cat. I called the police, who kept me on the phone and were about to send a car over when my mom came home from running an errand. Let me just say that I heard about that for a long time. However, I did identify with the terror of being home alone. Believe me, it was way before the movie and nothing like it. I knew what this kid was feeling.

All these thoughts ran through my head as I quietly spoke with the boy. Many things happened that night that are still with me to this day. I talked to an operator and asked her to trace the call. She told me that she had traced my call and was sending the police to investigate. That's all I'll say for now, but I will add that his mother did come home to find her child okay. She apologized and thanked us for staying on the phone with her son.

This incident got me thinking about one question in particular I asked the child: "Is there anyone or anything in the house with you?" He said that he was all alone. The boy in my story is not alone, which triggers a flashback in our hero to a time when he was not alone and was very afraid of someone or something. I would say that a lot of what transpires in the following story is the real deal.

BOOGIE

EXT: OFFICE BUILDING—NIGHT

Pieces of paper are blown in and around the office building by the seldom-felt cool breezes of a hot summer night. People in workday apparel slowly walk up and down the steamy sidewalks trying to shake off a week's worth of grime and stress. Up above, a single light burns in the night, symbolizing that not all of us are fortunate enough to leave our places of employment at the appointed time. The broom of a street cleaner pushes a pile of papers along the sidewalk. As the ash from his ever-present cigar falls into the papers, the smoke swirls up into the night sky, finding its way toward the light that burns. As the smoke gets closer to the window, the voice of a man is overheard.

VOICE

(very hurried)

... was that six orders of the one-eighteens or eight orders of the one-sixteens? ... Hold please ... Yes ... Ah no, they should have gone to Rochester, New York, not Rochester, Minn—Jesus Christ, up yours too, fella! Huh ... uh, I see ... well, how the hell am I supposed to know *that*?

INT: LEN'S OFFICE—NIGHT

The smoke travels inside the open window and introduces us to

LEONARD J. SMOOT, JR. He's a twenty-seven-year-old, brown-skinned black man, mustachioed, with a medium build. He is wearing a brown suit, somewhat rumbled, the jacket of which is thrown over a chair. The sleeves of his shirt are rolled up past his elbows. His tie hangs loosely around his neck like a hangman's noose. He is frantically punching at the blinking lights on his phone.

LEN

Excuse me, sir, I don't think that ... I'm sorry, what was that? Oh, pardon me, ma'am. Maybe you should try speaking in a higher voice. I don't think that cursing is the ... hey, hey. Oh yeah, well, right back at ya, lady. Try some hormones!

Len rolls his eyes and moves the phone to his other ear, while slowly punching another button on his overworked phone. As he talks, he attempts to write down some info with a cigarette, which breaks under the pressure of his frustrated finger.

LEN

Hello, Bangkok, Wisconsin ... What was that? ... Speak up, pal, I can't understand you. *What?* Thailand! Oh jeez, who's gonna pay for this? ... What? Oh, no thank you, I don't like my dog fried.

He slams the phone down hard and rubs his face, trying to wipe away the last eighteen hours of his life. He looks up to his extension ringing but hears no ringing. He picks up the phone.

LEN

Hello, hello, this is great. First I get into a fight with a transvestite and then I wind up ordering some dog McNuggets from Thailand and now my phone is out. My God, what else can happen?

Len starts to slam it down and remembers that it's broken and slowly sets the receiver down. He puts his head down on his desk and reflects on his life. He looks up at his framed and signed picture of Earl Graves, his hero.

LEN

Earl ... Earl, where did I go wrong? I know it's only been eight and a half months, but come on. One minute, I'm strokin' every chick on campus ... all right, maybe two. The next thing I'm working so much that I couldn't get phone sex from Dr. Ruth. See what happens when you listen to those god-damned guidance counselors? I bet they couldn't counsel a Girl Scout camp, let alone guide someone on their life. You know what they say: those who can't do, teach and those who can't do that, counsel.

INT: OUTER OFFICE AREA—NIGHT

His thoughts are interrupted by the arrival of two co-workers, both of whom he can't stand. BIFF, white, twenty-five years old, speaks to his buddy about his upcoming weekend.

                    BIFF
        How was the polo match last weekend? We should
        really rub their faces in it this time.

Biff spots Len's cubicle light on.

                    BIFF
        What do we have here? Our resident token burning
        the midnight oil. I bet he's using the company's
        phone to call one of his cousins or brothers or some-
        thing. Watch this, Daniel, ol' boy.

Biff picks up some folders from another desk and walks over to
Len's cubicle.

                    BIFF
        I say, ol' boy ... nothing personal, but I just wanted
        to say that you're doing a splendid job slaving away
        like you do. Excusez-moi, I didn't mean slaving—
        slip of the lip. Oh, by the by, I'll need these by Mon-
        day morning, in the a.m. before lunch, not the p.m.,
        old boy.

Before Len can react, Biff and his pal are off and laughing down
the hall. Len slouches in his chair, more depressed than ever.

LEN

That's just what I needed to top this day off: a visit from the jerk and his sidekick Mr. Off.

He glances up at his wall clock, Big Ben.

LEN

Its seven thirty and I'm here once again ...

He stands up in his tiny cubicle and looks over the tops of both sides of his portable walls and then slumps back down in his chair. He glances back up at Earl.

LEN

... Alone. Doesn't anyone else work at this damn company anymore? Okay, I admit that when I took this job they told me it wasn't going to be a piece of cake, but come on, Earl! I went to grade school, high school, college and grad school, and for what? I work eighteen hours a day, almost every weekend spent in this hole ... Jackasses like Biff and Biff, Jr. to contend with ... but wait, it gets better! The salesmen ... ahh, I *love* those guys. Get this, Earl: there are the old heads who have been with the company since Fred, Barney and the gang, and then there are the young boys who have the expense accounts and the company cars, but who are so inept that you end up covering their asses so the company doesn't lose the contracts!

He grabs the remaining reports that Biff had dropped off on his desk and throws them up in the air. As the papers fall through the air around him, he laughs.

LEN

I think it's time to call it a day.

He slowly rises from his squeaky chair and stretches. Just as he is about to grab his coat, the phone rings again. He decides to ignore it and finish closing up shop for the night. Just as he is about to head out the door he glances back the still ringing phone, then the clock, then the phone.

LEN

Damn ...

As he picks up the phone he realizes it may be Biff calling to give him more work to do.

LEN
(shouting)
Look here, Biffo, you jackass! I'm sick and tired of the shit you've been dishing out since I got here. Those junior execs you push around lick your ass every time you take a ...

He stops for a reaction from the Biffster, but hears nothing but a high-pitched breathing.

> LEN

Biff? ... Biff? ... Who is this?

Len hears the crying of a small child. He looks into the receiver as if to see who is on the other end. He smiles when he realizes who he thinks it is.

> LEN

Yo, David, is this you? You freak of nature ...I'm gonna kick your ass.

The breathing turns into a weeping of a small child. It causes him to stop in mid-sentence.

> LEN

Who is this?

> CHILD (OS)

I ... I want my mommy!

> LEN

Your mommy? ... Listen, kid—or whoever you are. I've had a hard week and some stupid-ass joke would really send me over the edge.

The child cries again, more intensely.

LEN

Whatever happened to the Mr. Clean in the bottle
jokes?

CHILD
(screaming)
I want my mommy! It's getting black outside. I'm
getting very scared.

Len rubs his face hard, as if trying to decide what to do. He
sighs.

LEN
(thinking out loud)
I must have done something in a past life to deserve
this ...

The child screams again, which causes Len to jump in his seat.

LEN
(surprised)
Jesus, kid, calm down ... OK, I'll help you.

The kid quiets to a whimper.

LEN
Now, that's better. Is there anyone home with you?

CHILD
(quietly)

Well, I ... yes.

LEN
(sighs)

Can you put them on the phone, please?

CHILD

Nnooo!

LEN

Why not?

CHILD

'Cuz my bear only talks to me.

LEN
(giving up)

Okay, fine.

CHILD
(innocently)

Have you seen my mommy? I want her *now*!

LEN

Well, tell me—does she work here?

CHILD

Yeah, she works real hard!

Len switches the phone to his other hand.

LEN

What's your mommy's name?

                         CHILD

Mommy.

                          LEN

What's her last name?

                         CHILD

Mrs. Mommy.

                          LEN

What's *your* name?

                         CHILD

Bobby, but my daddy calls me the Big Guy.

                          LEN

Well, listen, Big Guy, what's your last name?

                    BIG GUY (BG)

Conrad.

Len breathes a sigh of relief.

                          LEN

This may not be such a pain in the ass after all.

                          BG

                       (timidly)

Mr. Man?

                          LEN

You don't have to call me mister—my name is Leonard. I'm gonna look for your mommy in the company directory.

There is a moment of silence.

                    BG

I want my mommy. It's getting black outside and
the boogie is gonna come.

                    LEN

The boogie? What the hell is that? Come on, Big
Guy, there's no such thing as the boogie man. Did-
n't your daddy tell you that?

Nothing.

                    LEN

Big Guy?

                    BG

Yes, he does ... but I don't know ...

                    LEN

Okay, we'll get your mommy home as soon as possible.

                    BG

                 (still unsure)

Okaaay.

                    LEN

Now listen, I'm gonna put down the phone just for
a moment, okay?

                    BG

Nnooo!

Len pulls the phone from his ear. For the first time he feels that something could be wrong. A bead of sweat rolls down his fore-head.

LEN
(thinking out loud)
Jesus, what could this kid be so afraid of? Sure, the boogie man scared me, but I never screamed at it. I don't remember screaming...

INT: FLASHBACK/BASEMENT STAIRWAY
BLACK. Total darkness. The absent of all light and life. Or is it?

LEN'S FATHER (OC)
Lenny ... Lenny, get me another beer out of the fridge, will ya?
LEN, JR. (OC)
Daddy, I don't see any more in here.
FATHER (OC)
Shit ... Try downstairs in the basement. Hurry your ass up, the commercial's almost over and the deacon is about to take some white boys to Sunday school.

There's a click of a light switch and a ray of light shoots out from underneath the basement door. The door slowly creaks open, allowing incandescent light to invade the darkness. The silhouette of a small boy stands in the doorway. He leans for-ward, looking for something.

LEN, JR.

(trying to be brave)

My daddy says that you are a filament of
'magination ... and ... and he never lies, 'cept for the
time he told me that God could do anything, so ...

As Li'l Len talks, he very slowly moves down the steps. He picks
up one of the brooms that hang on the wall and slowly reaches
out and switches on the basement light. The lone bulb washes
the basement in an eerie light.

LEN, JR.

I asked God for a new rocky Roadster like Ethan,
my bestest friend got, and ... and guess what, I'm
still waiting.

He cautiously moves down the steps. From the shadows of the
basement, two red eyes follow his every move. Len, Jr. stops in
mid-step when he hears a guttural noise from the shadows. His
eyes focus on the eyes that watch him.

LEN, JR.

(very scared)

Kittyyy? Is that you? Be a good c-cat and c-come
here.

He hears several boxes start to move in the shadows. The
thought of the noise being his cat Phats calms him a bit, be-

cause she always comes to him when he calls.

LEN, JR.

You're a bad k-kitty for sscaring me like that. I'm gonna ...

He's interrupted by a purring from behind him. He turns to see Phats perched in the basement doorway.

LEN, JR.

Phats, how did you ...?

His attention is diverted by the noise of falling boxes, one of which hits the hanging bulb, casting bizarre and eerie images everywhere. In the shadows he sees something slowly moving toward the stairs. Terrified, he starts to move back up the stairs.

LEN, JR.
(scared witless)

Mmonster, Mmonster, g-go away ... Mmonster, Mmonster, sstay far away ...

Out of nowhere a hand shoots out of the shadows and grabs him by the shoulder, causing him to scream in terror.

INT: LEN'S CUBICLE—NIGHT

Len snaps back to reality. Sweat rolls down his face as he tries to shake off the memory. He returns his attention to the subject at hand.

LEN
(into the phone)
This sshouldn't take t-too long, so just hang on, okay?

Before the child can protest, he puts the boy on hold and quickly dials the company operator.

OPERATOR (OC, female, very nasal)
Operator Thirty-five, how can I be of assistance?
LEN
Yes, I'm looking for an employee named Conrad. A woman, most likely a Mrs.

There is a pause, then a sigh of apathy.

OPERATOR
(bothered)
Sir, did you know that it is after six p.m. on a Friday?
LEN
(annoyed)
Yeah, I'm aware of what time it is, the date and what country we are residing in. Do you want to know anything else?
OPERATOR
(snappy)
Sir, you don't have to get nasty. Besides, only an

emergency would warrant the acquisition of a home phone number.

LEN

Listen up, Evileen, I've got a scared kid on the other line who's looking for his mother. If you don't want to help him it will be on your head.

OPERATOR

Hey, I didn't know that there was a kid involved, and scared too. Okay, what was the name again?

LEN

Conrad.

OPERATOR

Conrad ... Conrad ... Here we go: Lisa Conrad. There's only one ... no Ms. or Mrs. though.

LEN

Great ... Let's have it ... uh, good, good ... thanks.

He writes down the number.

OPERATOR

Let me know how everything turns out ...

He puts down the receiver with a look of satisfaction. He quickly goes to the kid on the other line.

LEN

Big Guy, are you there?

All he hears is the high-pitched breathing.

BG
(really scared)

Where did you *go*? You promised that you wouldn't
go away. You promised the boogie wouldn't come!

LEN
(confused)

The boogie? What the hell are you talking about?

He can hear the kid running in place.

BG

He's upstairs! I can hear him!

He suddenly realizes he's involved in the worst kind of scenario.

LEN

Is there someone in the house with you?

BG

I told you that the boogie was here!

LEN

No, no not like the boogie ... like, mommy and
daddy.

BG

Nnooo ... but ...

He breathes a sigh of relief.

LEN

Thank you, God. Now, Big Guy, you have to listen
to me if we're going to get Mommy back home,
okay?

Silence.

LEN

Never, never put the phone down or hang it up.
Promise me.

BG

Are you mad at me?

LEN

No, I'm not mad, but promise me you won't, okay?

BG

Okay, I promise, and so does my bear.

LEN

Good boy. Now, how old are you, Big Guy?

BG
(proudly)

I'm these many ...

LEN

How many are these many? Can you count them?

BG
(proudly)

One, two, three, four ... five

57

LEN

Five years old. You're all grown up. No wonder your
daddy calls you the Big Guy.

The kid's attitude quickly changes to extreme fear.

BG

I sscared!

LEN

Big Guy, listen to me. When I was a big guy like you
I would tell my daddy that I was scared, and do you
know what he told me?

All he hears is the kid's labored breathing.

LEN

He told me the monster saying. Do you want to
hear it?

BG

Okay ... I guess.

LEN

Monster, monster go away. Monster, monster stay
far away.

BG

Did it keep the monster away?

LEN

Why, of course it did. I never saw one after I said it.
Do you think that you could say it? It will make you

feel better.

BG

Yeah ... Monster ... away ...

LEN

We'll say it together. Ready?

LEN/BG

Monster, monster go away. Monster, monster stay far away.

LEN

Don't you feel better? Now listen, I'm gonna put you on hold for a second so I can call your mommy.

BG

You promised!

LEN

Remember the monster saying? Do me a favor and turn on the TV. It'll keep you company till I get back.

He hears the TV snap on. In the background he hears the theme music to the *Twilight Zone*. He slowly puts him on hold.

LEN

Jesus Christ, what a minute. What the hell is the matter with me? I can wrap this up in a minute. If I call the number that Evileen gave me and it's busy it means that the kid is on the phone with me. Then I can get an address and call in the law and I'll be able to home in time for *Miami Vice*. Voilà, problem solved!

All those years of college *did* pay off.

Proud of himself, he dials the number and prays that it's busy. It rings.

                         LEN
Damn ...
                         VOICE
                  (female, older)
Hello.
                         LEN
Hi, my name is Leonard Smoot and looking for a Lisa Con—
                         VOICE
Well, she isn't here right now. Can I help you?
                         LEN
Let me ask you something. Does she have a son about five ...

                         VOICE
A what? A son? I *knew*. I just *knew* it. See, my corns always hurt when that tramp lies to me. She told me that she wanted to move out 'cuz she wanted to expand her horizons. Horizons, my ass. The only thing that's going to expand is her waistline. She's no daughter of mine ...

He holds the phone a little farther from his ear as the voice gets louder and louder.

LEN

But ... but ...

She doesn't miss a beat.

VOICE

But nothing! Hey, wait a goddamn minute. Is this the father? Listen here, you child molester, my baby was pure as the driven snow until you got your hot li'l whatever in her. And another thing—

He slowly hangs up the phone and rubs his face hard.

LEN

(thinking out loud)

All right, just take it easy. Plan A went down the tubes. Now it's time to call in the big gun, the bomb—Plan B ... Uh, what *was* plan B? Hmm ... oh yeah, it was that plan A had to work 'cuz there was no plan B. Why is this happening to me? I ate all my peas when I was a kid.

He puts his head down on the desk. His train of thought is broken when he remembers the Big Guy. He quickly picks up the phone, punches the line and hears the boy crying.

LEN

Are you there? What's wrong?

BG

(scared)

Monster, monster stay far away ... It's the boogie. I
can hear him and smell him. I told you, I told you ...

In the background Len hears a noise that triggers a memory/
dream.

INT: LEN, JR.'S BASEMENT—NIGHT

He is backing up the stairs with terror in his eyes. He stumbles.

LEN, JR.

Daddy! Please believe me! Don't you see it?

As he screams he leans back and sees the upside-down silhouette of his father standing in the doorway. The boy reaches out
for all he is worth, trying to grab his father's hand.

LEN, JR.

(frantic)

Daddy! Please, you promised, you *promised* ...

He sees his father reach out a hand to save him from the horror
down below. Len, Jr. grabs the hand, only to realize that it has
turned into a hideously deformed mass of flesh with a serious
set of claws.

INT: LEN'S CUBICLE—NIGHT

For the first time Len feels the hair on his neck stand on end.

> LEN

Whaat was that?

> BG

He's here, he's here! T-take me away.

> LEN

Something ... someone is after you?

> BG

Booogiiie!

After the boy's bone-chilling scream, Len hears the phone hit the floor.

> LEN
> (screams)

Big Guy!

He quickly grabs the other line and dials 911.

> OFFICER (OC)

Thirty-third precinct. What do you want? I mean, can I help you?

> LEN

I'd like to report a lost child!

> OFFICER

Okay, hold your water. Is this your child?

LEN

No, but ...

OFFICER

A relative?

LEN

No, I don't know him, but ...

OFFICER

Well, if you don't know, how can you claim that he's lost? Guido, is this you?

LEN

Guido? No, my name's Leonard Smoot and I have a lost kid on the phone who's in trouble ...

OFFICER

Trouble! Why didn't you say so? What kind of trouble?

LEN

Deep trouble.

OFFICER

How deep is deep?

LEN

Would you believe ... the boogie man?

OFFICER

Jesus H. Christ, whatever happened to the Mister Clean in the bottle joke?

The cop hangs up hard.

LEN
(screams into the phone)
No ... no ... don't do that! This isn't a joke! Don't
you understand it's the goddamn boogie man and it
has a kid!

He slams the phone down in utter frustration. Breathing hard
and sweating, he stares at the phone. He quickly reaches for the
phone and punches the line that the Big Guy is on. The light
continues to blink.

LEN
Hello, hello! The kid is depending on me and damn
phone breaks again.

He screams at the top of his lungs out of frustration. He winds
down and stares at the blinking light. All at once he has a
thought and runs out of his cubicle to ...

INT: BULLPEN/NEXT CUBICLE—NIGHT

... the bullpen, looking for something. His eye catches the glimmer
of a blinking light coming from the receptionist's phone.
He dives for it.

LEN
Big Guy!

He listens and hears the whimpering of a small child.

> LEN
>
> Are you there? Are you all right?

There is a long pause.

> BG
>
> It hurts ... It hurts ...

Tears of fear roll down Len's face.

> LEN
>
> It hurts? *What* in God's name hurts?

All he hears is the phone hitting the floor again. Without thinking, he puts the call on hold and dials nine and zero.

> OPERATOR (OC)
>
> How can I help you?
>
> LEN
>
> I'd like to have a number traced. It's a matter of life and death!
>
> OPERATOR (OC)
>
> Did you say trace a call? What do you think this is, *Miami Vice* or something? Let me guess—you're Cockett, right?

LEN

Please, you've got to help me; no one else will. It's on the other extension. It's a kid and he's in trouble and the boo—and something is after him!

OPERATOR

Jesus, all right already. I've only been here a short time. Let me get my supervisor.

A moment passes while the connection is made.

SUPV (OC)

I'm told that you would like a trace made, sir.

LEN

Yes, it's a matter of life and death.

SUPV

In order to make a trace, I am required to get your number and current address from which you are calling.

LEN

My address? I know where *I* am. I'm trying to locate a—

SUPV

Sir, it is mandatory by law to get the address of the requestee. Now, that number and address please.

LEN

(giving up)

Okay, you win. 1872 Riverside Drive, third floor. My number is 555-1793, but I still don't understand—

                    SUPV

Listen, punk, do you know that it is a federal offense
to play with the phone company, especially for
punks like you who get their rocks off by making
prank calls?

Len is caught off guard.

                    LEN

A *prank*? What the hell are you talking about?

                    SUPV

As we speak a patrol car is on its way to pick you up.

                    LEN

Pick me up! I'm not the one in trouble. It's him, the
boy!

                    SUPV

Dramatic, aren't we? Tell it to the judge.

Len is almost in tears. Before he hangs up, the operator he had
spoken with before comes back on.

                  OPERATOR

I heard it all. She's a bitch. I don't know if I should
do this, but you seem real to me so I traced the call.
Here's the number: 555-2977. The address is 280
Clearview Drive.

He closes his eyes.

> LEN
>
> That's pretty close to here. Thank you, God.
>
> OPERATOR
>
> Uh-oh. Here she comes with blood in her eyes.

Before he can thank her she hangs up. He looks at the still-blinking line that the Big Guy is still on and makes a decision. He runs out of the office and down the stairs.

EXT: MAIN ENTRANCE/BUILDING—NIGHT

A policeman is walking backward to the main entrance. He speaks to his partner, who is in the patrol car.

> OFFICER #1
>
> Look, Carl, it will only take a minute. You don't have to tell me that we get all the shit calls. It's your fault. You're the one who thought the sarge would like a little slap and tickle.

The policeman walks through the swinging door as Len comes flying out of it. He sees the officer on the ground but keeps running as he hits the street.

OFFICER #2 opens his door and runs after Len.

EXT: STREET—NIGHT

OFFICER #2

Stop in the name of the law!

Len doesn't hear the copper and keeps running. At one point the cop gets close enough to make his move. He dives, but Len zigs, causing him to hit a bunch of trashcans.

EXT: CLEARVIEW DRIVE—NIGHT

He finally comes to the corner of Clearview Drive and turns up onto the street. His mind wanders as he runs, sending back to his nightmare.

INT: BASEMENT/FLASHBACK—NIGHT

Len, Jr. lies at the bottom of the steps trying to get up. The lone light casts shadows everywhere. All at once the terror stops. The lights and sounds return to normal. The boy sighs.

LEN (VO)

No! Can't relax! Run, goddamn it, run!

Len, Jr. starts up the stairs again. Out from underneath the steps shoot two monstrous, hairy, sore-ridden arms, which grab the boy's ankles. He holds on to the banister, trying to regain his balance. Another inhuman hand bursts through the wall, latching on to the shoulder of its victim. As the boy in the flashback screams, so does the present-day Len.

EXT: CLEARVIEW DRIVE—NIGHT

The screaming of another little boy brings him back to reality. He turns, looking for the origin of the pleas. Out of the corner of his eye he sees a flash of light. Like a moth drawn to a flame, he runs to the eerie light. It's the house. As he runs he is cut off by a police car that skids to a stop in front of him, sending him over the hood. The two cops from before jump out, slam him onto the hood and cuff him. They spin him around and punch him in the stomach, dropping him to his knees. At that moment a MAN and WOMAN walk up carrying a load of groceries.

MAN

What's the meaning of this?

OFFICER #1

This suspect was running from the police. He said something about a kid in trouble ...

As the officer explains, the woman turns toward her house to see the door slowly opening. She screams as the Big Guy, (seven years old, black) walks out into the night air. His shirt has been slashed and is spotted with blood. He carries a teddy bear with him.

BIG GUY

Monster, monster go away ... Monster, monster stay far away ... You promised ...

Len mouths the words that the boy is saying. Breaking free from the police, Len runs to the Big Guy and falls at his feet.

LEN

I'm sorry ...

At this point everyone runs up and surrounds Len and the boy. His mom scoops him up. The Big Guy drops his bear to the ground.

EXT: HOUSE—NIGHT

Some time has passed, and the police have arrived in full force. Len has been released from the cuffs and is listening to a DE-TECTIVE try to explain what happened to the distraught parents. The group is standing some distance from the house.

DET

Well, the way we see it, it was a large dog of some kind that got into the house. Your son seems a little traumatized but unharmed ...

The kid sits between his parents as if in some of trance. The supervisor pats the kid on the head to emphasize his point. Big Guy remains motionless, occasionally leaning forward from between his parents to peer at the house.

DET

Yeah, anyway, your son says that the boogie man

had something to do with this ...

Len surveys his surroundings and feels as if something is listening and watching him. He turns and looks at the house. He sees a cop standing at the front door, but nothing else is out of the ordinary. He moves toward the front door. The Big Guy leans forward, watching him. The cop at the door speaks to Len.

OFFICER #2

I'll be damned if my kid doesn't blame everything on the boogie man. Get this: he even screams out in the middle of the night. Kids say the goddamndest things, right, Mr.Smoot?

Len is concentrating on the house, not really listening to the cop.

LEN

Yeah ... the damndest things.

Len looks back at the kid and then back at the house. They both look scared to death.

OFFICER #2

Mr. Smoot, I hope that there are no hard feelings. You know, me pushing you around and all before.

Len ignores the apology. The officer gives him a shrug and walks away. He looks up into the darkened house.

INT: HOUSE—NIGHT
He hears a low rustling and goes inside, moving slowly, tentatively. He stands in the foyer and looks around. He walks to the base of the steps and peers up them. He realizes that the kid may have just fallen down the steps.

                    LEN
He must have imagined the whole thing. Maybe his folks don't listen to him enough or something. It must be tough being home alone.

EXT: HOUSE—NIGHT
Len walks out of the house and over to the boy.

                    LEN
So how are you feeling, Big Guy?
                    BG
Okay, I guess.
                    LEN
You ripped your shirt pretty good. Well, I guess we beat the stuffin' out of that old boogie.

As Len talks to him he glances back to the house, into the shadows, into the darkness. His voice trails off; he's searching for the boogie. The Big Guy reaches up and puts a hand on Len's cheek. Len snaps out of his trance.

LEN

Listen, I know what it's like to be scared. Even bigger guys like me are afraid sometimes. And it's even worse when there is no one to help you out. You know what I mean?

The Big Guy nods.

LEN

But when you do, we know what you have to say to make everything okay, right?

The Big Guy jumps into Len's arms and hugs him tightly.

BG

You did it! You saved me ...us.

LEN

Everything is gonna be okay. We both know what to say to it to make it go away, right? Besides, it's just a filament ... I mean *figment* of your imagination.

The boy nods. Len strolls over to the side of the house to lean against a tree and watch as the police are winding up their investigation.

LEN

(singing)

Monster, monster go away ...

In mid-sentence two huge hairy arms reach down
and grab Len by the head and quickly pull him up
into the tree. A snapping of bone is heard.

CREDIT SEQUENCE.

Chapter 4

YIN AND YANG

"My son is the bridge that separates good from evil."
—Sarge

INTRODUCTION

One of the first true writing jags I can remember experiencing happened while I was in Stamford, Connecticut. A lot of it had to do with trying to build up a quick catalog of work to show a prospective agent. I was being booked to work in Connecticut on various shows at a production facility. I was still living on Ocean Ave in Brooklyn, so the commute was a bitch. First, I'd have to jump on the D train ...

Let me stop here for a moment, because it's time for a word about my beloved D train. I was fortunate enough, or so I'm told, to have found a place to live a month after moving to NYC. I was staying with an uncle of a girlfriend when I got up one day and decided to find an apartment. I found it that day, right down the street. It was my first spot out of college and I was glad to get it. I thought I was lucky to have the Prospect Park Subway Station right under my bedroom window. At its worst, I remember calling the MTA telling them to please shut off the loudspeaker announcing that the train was on time and if you had any problems please call us. Of course this came out as something no one could understand, but after hearing it three hundred times you come to know it by heart. At least I didn't have to look up the phone number. I had it timed to where I could hear the train coming and run out of my building, around the corner, through the turnstile, down the steps and onto the subway. When it worked it was a thing of beauty, but when it didn't ... well, I'll just say it was frustrating.

Anyway, my journey to Stamford began on the D train. I got off at the 42nd Street stop and transferred to the 7 train. I got off at Grand Central Station and jumped on the Metro North Train to Stamford. Once there I would catch a taxi to the production facility. Door to door it was roughly one and a half hours one way. I know that some of you are saying: "What's he complaining about? One and a half hours ain't no hardship. Man up, motherfucker!"

Well, my friends, the problem was not in riding three trains and a taxi; it was in the timing.

I guess I'm telling you all this to explain how I wound up staying in the Stamford Marriott Hotel the majority of the time I worked there. I was lucky to have employers who would put me up most of the time in this hotel when a shoot went late into the night. I also had a very good friend, Leonard, who put me up when I was low on cash. I would have people over from time to time to hang out. I remember there was this one secretary who worked for the facility. I really liked her. We would hang out and I would let her read what I was writing. She liked the way I put everyday brand-name objects into my stories. I got this from reading a lot of Steven King. It somehow added a higher sense of reality no matter what the circumstances. The product that comes to mind was Spider-man Underoos. You might remember them—they were PJ's a lot of kids wore in the '80s. Anyway, I told her that I'd write a story for her. It was close to Christmas, so every store had their decorations out. I remember walking around town taking in the holiday spirit and coming across a toy store. The hit toys that season were the Transformers that were based on the cartoon series. They seemed almost alive to me. This idea turned into a series of thoughts, and before I knew it I was Dream Thinking.

Okay, now I'll be the first to admit I thought it might help my "cause," so I wrote *Yin and Yang* for her. All I'll say is that I didn't get the girl in the end but I did get an interesting story out of it. Yes, I know it's not the same thing, but give a brother a break.

YIN AND YANG

Since the death of Paul's father, his mother noticed that her five -year-old son had retreated further and further into himself. All the books said that this was a normal reaction to the lost loved one. Even Joan Lunden on *Mothers' Minutes* said that sometimes small children have to come to grips with death in their own time and way. One day Paul came bouncing out of his bedroom, just like he had done million times before the passing of his father. He was talking a mile a minute while he ate his Campbell's chunky soup. After he finished his dinner, he bounded off his high chair and ran into his room.

"Don't play for too long, Paul," she said, with a familiar smile from days gone by. The death of her husband had hit her hard. Real hard. One day he had gone off to his job at Shangi International Toys and disappeared ... no body ... no nothing. The police didn't know what to think, but after six months the only thing to think was that he'd died.

Her thoughts were interrupted by Paul talking in his room. It was strange, because she and her son were the only people in the house. She walked up to the door and placed her ear to the wood.

Okay, Daddy ... I'll go and pick it up for you ... Yes, I promise, I do! ... Don't go, I miss you so much!"

Mrs. Jensen opened the door to see her son alone in his room with his green army men set up as if at attention. "What the hell is going on here?" she asked.

Paul sat there staring at his WWII army men, and then slowly turned toward his mom. "It's okay, Mommy," he said, smiling. "Daddy said so."

She stood there with her mouth agape as her son walked by her.

"I'll get it," he said, a moment before the doorbell rang. He ran toward the living room. Mom followed slowly and went to the window to look outside. She saw her son picking up a package that had been left on the steps. Looking up at the sky, she saw a storm gathering. Paul looked up at the window and saw his mom looking at him. He smiled and quickly ran back into the house. Once inside, he went straight to his room. As he walked past her, he stopped and held up his bounty. She grabbed it from him, but the box was heavy and she dropped it. Out of the box fell two or three one-foot-high creatures with albino skin and blood-red eyes. She screamed, but then realized that they were just toys. Paul went over and picked them up and carefully placed them back in the box. He started off toward his room. When Mom got her shit together, she followed her son into his room. He proceeded to set the creatures up opposite his carefully placed army men.

"Where did those things come from?" she asked.

Without looking up, Paul answered: "From Daddy's company. He told me that they were coming." Mom leaned forward, watching him carefully.

"Daddy? You mean before he ... uh, went away?" she asked.

"You mean died? Yeah," said Paul. He turned his attention back toward the ugly creatures. "Daddy told me to call them Gories," he told her.

An apt name, Mom thought. They were indeed gory looking, with their large, hairless bodies and small heads. When Paul had unpacked all of them, she noticed that the army men and the Gories were equal in number, though the Gories were immense in comparison.

"I'm tired, Mommy. Going to bed now." She watched as her son undressed himself and put on his Spider-man Underoos. When he finished, Paul went over to her and hugged her real hard. Her mind traveled back to the morning her husband left for work for the last time. He too had hugged her tightly, as if to say goodbye. She snapped out her flashback when her son pulled away from her. Telling herself her imagination was getting away from her, she kissed him on the forehead and tucked him into bed.

At precisely midnight, a bolt of lightning exploded near the house, followed by several more. The only things disturbed by this force of nature were the toys. Each lightning strike illuminated the scene, and an observer would have seen a slight movement in the limbs of the creatures and the army men. Slowly, one by one, they came alive and moved about. The Gories' eyes started to glow a bright blood red as they came alive. They scattered among the (to them) oversized furniture in the child's room. The army men came alive and tried to regroup, but were ambushed by the waiting Gories. They quickly dove for cover. For a brief moment nothing happened. The stillness had the edge of a newly sharpened Ginsu blade. Sergeant York, the platoon leader, peeked up over an Adidas sneaker and locked eyes with the leader of his mortal enemy. The creature let out an inhuman scream. "Eat 'em up, boys! Boo! Yaaa!"

The darkness was lit up by the gunfire from their weapons. In response, the Gories fired back with spears and flying discs. WWIII began that night in a little boy's room. Cry havoc and let loose the dogs of war.

During a break in the fighting, York called his men to rally behind the Castle Grayskull toy set. He went through the roll: "Johnson, Peewee, Washington, Sparks, Jojo, Sampson, Doc and Junior."

"Sarge, Junior got grabbed from behind as soon as the firefight started. He put up a good fight but the thing was too much for him."

Out of the darkness they heard a high-pitched screaming: "Hhheeelllp mmeee!" It was Junior. Several of them made a move to help their fallen comrade, but the sergeant stopped them.

"No one move a fuckin' muscle. Youse guys will be picked off like ticks on a whore in this darkness. Plus, they can see in the dark," the sarge said, stopping his men in their tracks.

"Who or ... what in the hell *are* those things, Sarge?"asked Sparks.

"Huddle up, guys. Men, we have been chosen for a mission that could change the course of both man- and toy kind as we now know it. Those things, those Gories out there are here for one thing and one thing only: to kill my son," he said wearily.

"If he dies tonight, we and all other toys that represent all that is good will perish. Our destruction will open a trans-universal doorway, allowing Hell to run amok in this dimension. My son is the bridge that separates good from evil."

At that moment, a disc came flying out of the darkness and hit Washington in the chest. The rest of the men dropped to the floor. Doc crawled over to Washington and wept: Washington was gone. The men regrouped and decided on a plan of action. Before they could act, however, the eyes of the Gories began to glow. A wall of red light illuminated the room, and just as quickly dissipated. Johnson saw one of them on top of a fire truck, ready to throw a spear. He took aim and fired. Nothing but a click. All the men tried to fire their weapons, but none of them worked.

"What the fuck happened?" Sparks asked, trying to fix his machine gun.

"It must have been that light they generated. They shut us down," Doc answered.

"The hell they have," Sarge said, looking around. He picked up a paperclip and bent it into a crude boomerang. Before he could throw it, a Gory jumped out and heaved a spear at him. Without thinking, Sarge threw the boomerang to Jojo, caught the spear, and in one fluid motion hurled it right back at the Gory, whose large, hairless gray body was cut in two. Jojo saw another one climbing up the blinds and launched the boomerang, hitting it in the back of its neck. It fell to the floor in a heap. Without missing a beat, Sarge sent his men out to look for materials for weapons. They came back with paperclips, rubber bands and matches. Sampson fashioned a crude bow and arrow out of a paperclip and a rubber band. Striking a match on the floor, he spied a Gory running right at him. Taking aim, he fired the arrow, hitting the Gory and igniting it. It fell into a goldfish bowl, putting out the flames.

Sarge grabbed the bow when he saw a Gory on the bedpost above his son. As it leapt into the air, he fired. The unlit match ignited in midflight due to friction, hitting it square in the back. The Gory screeched in pain and vaporized. The air was suddenly filled with flying discs and spears. Doc was hit in the leg and went down. Sampson dragged him to safety.

Sarge told Peewee to go high to get a better view of the battle zone. Using a grappling hook, he threw it up to the second shelf of a bookcase and quickly scampered up the line with the grace of a gymnast. Out of the darkness a Gory came swinging on a rope, clenching a knife in its sharpened teeth. Peewee jumped to another shelf and the Gory just missed him, hitting the edge of the shelf. This sent the knife blade completely through its skull. He signaled to his comrades that the enemy was closing in on the bed where the Sarge's son was sleeping. Sarge ordered his men to fan out around the base of the bed and protect the boy at all costs. However, as they rounded the corner of the bed, they were ambushed. The next several moments were some of the most intense hand-to-hand combat ever seen. Peewee joined his comrades in arms in the battle.

When the smoke cleared, the Sarge and the head Gory, Pluto, were the only two left standing. Pluto leapt over Sarge, landing on the bed and running toward the child to finish his unholy mission. Sarge, who was wounded, watched helplessly as the Gory got closer and closer to his son. He looked around the room, desperate for a way to get up there. Then he saw it: a jack-in-the-box. Getting on top of it, he pressed the button and launched himself through the air. Seeing that that Pluto was lifting a spear to throw into his son's ear, he twisted his body, changing his trajectory. He landed on the bed and bounced at the Gory, hitting him with a cross-body block and sending them both to the edge of the bed. As they hung there, Sarge looked over at Pluto to see his blood-red eyes staring at him. Pluto shook his head as if to say "You lose," and pulled himself back onto the bed. The battle-weary father climbed back up to see Pluto holding the spear. The Gory smiled, knowing that it had won. Sarge let out a cry of desperation. At that exact moment, though, the first rays of sunlight shone through the window, hitting the Gory. His body started to smoke and then vaporized into nothing but a bad dream.

Paul awoke from his slumber to find his room a mess. He turned his head to see a lone army man lying on the pillow. He picked it up and hugged it tightly.

"Thanks, Daddy," he murmured. "I knew you could do it."

Chapter 5

KILLER BUSH

"I'm a savior, not a destroyer ... A savior."
—Willy

INTRODUCTION

From time to time I get into a serious exercise jag. I keep at it for six months or so before I revert to my evil ways. This particular jag took place when I was living in Brooklyn on Ocean Ave. The only nice thing I remember about this apartment was that I was right across the street from Prospect Park. This is a huge park with many hills and valleys. It was built for jogging. Out of all the exercises that you can choose, they say running or swimming give you the most bang for your buck. Since I wasn't near water (and by the way, I wouldn't recommend swimming in any natural water sources in Brooklyn) I decided to take up running and put the rubber to the road.

The other thing about Prospect Park is that during the day it was a wonderful place to hang out. Folks playing soccer, families out on picnics, concerts in the band shell—the full monty. At night, however, it changed into something else. Strange noises abounded. Screams cut the darkness like a knife. It's like the song says: "The freaks come out at night."

For the most part I stayed out of the park at night. I do remember one time wanting to run really bad and I couldn't wait till the morning light. Let me explain that for those of you who don't run: there is a plane of reality or hyper-reality you reach when running over a long period of time. Some call it runner's high, where the endorphins released into your brain stem alter your emotional state. It's like a drug. They say that once you break this barrier, your body, mind and soul crave it. Well, I had achieved this state and I needed to run. I knew it wasn't a good idea, but I found myself standing in front of the park entrance in my running gear. I stretched and thought about what I was going to do. Before I knew it my legs were moving and I was on my way. I will say that I ran around that park faster than I ever had before. I did hear some strange noises, but they just made me run faster.

Something that happened toward the end of that run ... something I will never forget. I had run all the way around the park and slowed to cool off by walking a bit. I was out of breath and my body and legs ached. I could see the entrance to the park and felt safe. Just then I heard a noise, and turned to see a stray cat run into a huge bush. I heard that cat let out a scream from the center of the bush that still brings the hairs on my nape to attention. I sprinted to the entrance of the park and up into my apartment.

That next morning I ran through the park as usual. When I got to the bush in question I slowed to a walk and looked at it. It didn't look the same to me. Somehow it seemed different. I never looked at that bush the same way again.

I used this experience to write "The Killer Bush." I took a tongue-in-cheek approach and expanded on it. Check it out ...

KILLER BUSH

It was always a big production number when the Smallville Psychiatric Center received a new member. The patient looked around at his new environment with a sense of belonging. The good thing about this patient was that he knew that he was crazy as a shithouse rat. They brought him into cell seven, or "lucky seven," as the orderlies liked to call it.

Inside sat an old man who never once looked up at his new roomie. He was dressed in a well-fitted jacket with matching pants. His eyes were dark and puffy from lack of sleep.

When everything was put away, the old man said, "You know, I'm a savior, not a destroyer."

"Is that right?" I said under my breath. Well, I must have said something right because he went on to tell me a tale that rocked my world.

On an average morning in an average town slept an average drunk on his favorite bench in the Town Park. We'll call our hero Willy. He was sleeping off the effects of a tough night's work. People jogged past him as they did every morning. The park attendants went about their business picking up refuse from picnics past.

This particular morning there was a slight difference in the air. It was not something that you could see, smell or hear, but something was definitely different. Willy woke from his morning nap and felt that something was out of whack. He looked around to see if anyone else had noticed the change. Before you could say "hoochie mama," he spied a bush that hadn't been there yesterday when he settled in for the night. About thirty feet from Willie's favorite bench, across the service road, sat a huge bush. Well, Willy didn't quite know what to make of the new addition to his park. It looked harmless enough. However, something was not right. After a few moments, he realized what it was: There wasn't an animal or bird on or near that bush the entire time that he looked at it. From out of the blue, scaring the snot out of him, a cat ran past Willy and right into the waiting bush. Willy heard a hissing, followed by a bone-crunching snap. Willy rubbed his eyes to hear better. Moments later, a park attendant wandered over to the bush to pick up a piece of paper near its base. When he stabbed the paper with his sticker, a strange-smelling white mist shot out of the bush, hitting him square in the kisser. When the mist cleared the man was holding the sticker like a spear. The thing that really scared Willy was the maniacal grin the man had on his face. It was almost a bloodlust of some kind.

Just at that moment, a jogger came around the corner of the park and ran past the waiting park attendant. Measuring his prey, the attendant hurled the javelin-like projectile into the back of the jogger. The jogger crashed to the ground and the attendant quickly ran over like a lion after a fresh kill and began to drag the still-twitching body toward the waiting bush. Right before he threw the body into the bush, several other joggers round the same corner to see what was going on. They ran over to get a closer look and the attendant attacked them like a man possessed. A cop car happened to be cruising by. Seeing on the disturbance, the cop hit his lights and siren and came to screeching halt. Once he saw that the men were not playing around, the cops jumped out and subdued the bunch of them. The joggers pointed to the legs of the first jogger sticking out from beneath the bush. When they pulled the body out, they saw that all that was left of him was his lower half. Several people fainted. The park attendant tried to make a break for it and was shot in the back. Willy, who had seen the chain of events from the beginning, screamed and fainted.

When he woke, he was looking into the face of police officer Frank Friendly, who was holding smelling salts. Friendly asked Willy if he had seen anything. Willy proceeded to tell the officer that the bush had sprayed the attendant with some kind of mist ray that caused him to go crazy. The police officer asked him about the missing body parts. "The bush ate them," Willy told him. The officer slowly took a seat on the bench next to the still-trembling Willy. He saw the empty liquor bottles on the ground. He told him that they could really use his help on this one and being smashed was not helping the situation one bit. As the police backed up their CSI gear, Willy pleaded with them to check out the bush.

That night, Willy stayed straight for once to wait for the bush to do something. For hours he lay huddled on the bench, watching the bush. Nothing happened. In the morning, just before he was about to nod off, two joggers came around the corner. The bush zapped them with the white mist. They commenced to beat the tar out of each other. Willy watched in horror as one jogger threw the other one into the jaws of the killer bush. Willy covered his ears, trying to drown out the screams and sounds of crunching bone. The killer jogger, who was still under the control of the bush, looked around for other victims. He spied Willy and started running toward him. In the nick of time, a cop on horseback spotted the wild man running through the park with blood on his clothing and intercepted the jogger in mid-leap.

After things calmed down a bit, the police questioned Willy again and basically got the same story. They got pissed off and left.

That night Willy decided that it was his mission in life to destroy the killer bush. He stole a gas can and some gasoline, and bummed some matches. He double-checked his gear like Rambo in *First Blood, Part II*. When everything was in working order, he set his plan into motion. When it got dark and the moon and several streetlights were the only things lighting his way he proceeded to his destination, quickly running from tree to tree till he could see the bush in the moonlight. Just as he was about to throw the gasoline into the bush, a hand came out of nowhere, stopping him. It spun him around, knocking him to the ground. He looked up to see Officer Friendly standing over him. The officer told Willy that he had taken it upon himself to stake out the bush to see what was really going on here. Willy told him that he was here to destroy his sworn enemy. Willy begged the officer to let him prove that the bush was evil. Friendly smiled and told Willy that he knew where the real evil was. Willy relaxed, thanking God that someone finally believed him. He turned to thank the officer, but saw a maniacal grin on his face and blood running down his chin. Friendly picked up the gas can, lifting it over his head to clobber Willy. The gas from the open can streamed down the officer's arms. Before he could bring the can down in a deathblow, Willy lit one of the matches and set the officer on fire. Friendly staggered around, and finally fell to the ground, a charred husk. As Willy watched in horror, he felt something snake around his ankle. The bush had sent out a branch to entangle Willy and pull him in for dinner. Willy realized what was going on. Picking up the half-empty gas can, he threw it at the bush. It landed short, but because of the downward slope of the ground the gas slowly rolled toward the bush. As the bush dragged him closer, Willy struggled to light the last match. He got it lit, but it went out when he tried to throw it at the gas trail. Looking frantically around, he happened to see a stray packet of matches about ten yards away. He rolled toward them, still in the grasp of the killer bush, and barely reached them in time. He quickly lit the match and the gas, setting it on fire. The bush let go of him and he ran like a man possessed. The bush let out a deafening, inhuman scream that included all the souls of the people it killed. It exploded into the night like the Fourth of July.

Several hours later, the police arrested Willy for the brutal murder of Officer Friendly and for destroying public property. As they led him away, he told them that he was a savior, not a destroyer. They put a muzzle on him. As he was carried off he saw a strange bush.

From that point on, the old man only repeated the same phrase over and over: "I'm a savior, not a destroyer. A savior, not a destroyer ..."

Chapter 6
A Random Dream Thought ...

HIBERNATION

It dreams of a different time.

It dreams of flying through the skies with its brothers and sisters, claiming the skies as their own. They would fill the skies with their hybrid forms, blocking out the sun.

It had no rivals in its world. Oh, at first in their early evolution before the wings of justice and the bonding, they were just another species to be eaten by the larger, more powerful animals ... but all that changed when it made the conscious decision to rise up out of the murky and dangerous depths of the seas.

At first their numbers were decimated by every walking creature with a need to feed. But then, over a period of eons, things changed—either by nature or by their own accord. These changes were created by not only eating and absorbing another species' DNA but by raping and impregnating other species with its seed. The young ones were looked after with the greatest of care so as not to destroy the next step in their growth.

It did not know why it did this, but it continued this process for generations upon generations. It went from a one-celled creature of the seas to walking on land, to the trees ... but then, in the third cycle, it all changed.

One spring day several hundred thousand of them dug into the ground and went to sleep. When they awoke and freed themselves from the earthly tombs, they continued on without missing a step. When the next generation was born something was different. They had wings, razor-sharp incisors, claws ... and something special: a hollow tongue with a calcium point that could penetrate any skull or bone mass.

The wings of Justice were born on that day.

It would hunt in packs, herding dinosaurs into valleys of death. Then the feasting would begin. At first they attacked in a disorganized manner, often fighting among themselves, killing off the weaker of its kind. Then one day one of them connected with the others via telepathy and things changed forever.

You see, the bonding had started.

That was when the true feasting began.

Even the most vicious species were wiped out within a generation. Compies, raptors, and the *T. rex* were gone before their small brains realized what was happening.

The newborns would feed on the bones until there was nothing left but gristle. However, their food source was soon diminished. You see, it was a greedy species, killing not only to eat but for the sport of it.

When there was nothing left to eat it dug back into the ground and went into its first hibernation.

Over a million of them are sleeping around the planet, waiting for it to replenish it itself. They are restless again. Their stomachs empty from slowly feeding off the last of their digested foodstuffs. Throughout time several have awoken to see if the new world is ready for their kind ...

Ready for the feasting.

When the scouts do not return with news or food, it is not time. When they had returned to the earth they learned that their kind had been glimpsed by humankind throughout the centuries. Humankind had made their kind into icons: the phoenix, the gargoyle, the griffin and many others.

However, something has changed. One of them has returned with something new; something that is smart like them and, best of all, delectable to the taste buds.

Humankind is the answer to their problem. They play with them at first, testing them to see their intelligence at work. Oh, they are smart all right! Maybe too smart, but that's part of the game.

This species is the dominant force on the planet and has never had a predator more powerful than itself. Stupidly, they have turned on themselves, for whatever reason.

This is not logical, but all that will change soon enough.

Learning from their past mistakes, they have decided to herd and farm this species so as to keep a fresh supply of meat and bone for future generations.

... It is time.

Chapter 7

BY ANY MEANS ...

"Musicians were forced to play on the
Musical Underground Railroad."
—Narrator

INTRODUCTION

For two summers in the mid-1980s I worked as assistant production manager for a summer concert series held on the pier in
NYC. Basically, I was a gofer. I cleaned the towels and ran er-
rands. The good part was this: I got my friends in for free. It
wasn't a bad deal. I looked good to my friends, getting them
into the VIP section, giving them free brew and allowing them
to hang out at the after parties with the artists. My boss had no
idea. I would get the VIP list, and as I walked it over to the security gate I would slip my list in too. It was foolproof ... until the
day the head of security took my list to my boss. I was caught
red-handed. I felt like shit for doing this behind his back. He
gave me a good talking to and let it go. Thank God.

One day Steel Pulse was playing at the venue. I called a
friend of mine, Cyril St. Aubun (by the way, one of the coolest
guys I know), and invited him to the show. He told me that he

knew several of the band members. I saw an opportunity here and told him that if I wrote a movie for them could he hook up a meeting? Cyril smiled and said that he could. I wrote like crazy for two days and came up with a film treatment. I gave the idea to them. Over the next couple weeks I spoke to them in England, and they told me that they were coming to NYC again. I got a producer friend of mine, Joel Hinman, to agree to produce the project for me. He got a hotel room at the Plaza. Things fell apart, thought, when they found out Joel was white and thought that I was going to take advantage of them. The project died an ugly death.

The spark for the idea came from watching Tipper Gore testifying in senate hearings on banning certain types of music. I asked myself: "What if they did ban certain types of music? Wouldn't reggae be the first one banned?" I just took it from there. Using the films *Fahrenheit 451* and *1984* as jumping-off points, I created a world where musical creativity was not only discouraged, but outlawed.

BY ANY MEANS ...

As the dragon squad walks up the stairs, they are careful not to make any noise. The journey up the narrow stairwell seems to take an eternity. Everyone in the group flinches when the soft, lyrical sounds of reggae cut through the air like a knife. The point man of the elite British police tactical unit halts his group at the top of the stairs. As he peeks over the top step, he sees bluish smoke billow from underneath the closed door. The sweet-smelling smoke engulfs him and his men like a cheap suit. He quickly covers his nose and turns to see several of his men take in deep mouthfuls of the intoxicating mist.

After the smoke clears the lieutenant waves his hand, sending four of his men to take positions around the door. All at once the men rush the door, which crashes under their weight. Several moments pass. The squad is momentarily stunned as the smoke clears, revealing the scene before them. Inside the room, a group of black men are playing to four or five families crowded into the cramped flat. Without missing a beat the squad pulls and pushes the families apart, trying to get at the musicians. The police use excessive force to subdue the band. As they leave, the commander looks back and surveys the work he and his men have done. The room looks as if a tornado has passed through it. Several people are screaming in pain, including a small girl crying out for her now-dead parents.

Outside, the renegades are brought before the waiting press.

The flashlights and bright lights all but blind the newly captured prisoners. Off to one side of the pandemonium, the official government reporter says that after five years of being on the run and playing their music, the most wanted band in the world, Steel Pulse, has be subdued. The long, intense battle resulted in the death of fifteen people, five of whom were children. The musicians committed all of these fatalities. All this was captured on tape and will be sold as a DVD compilation Christmas limited edition. The commander of the Dragon Squad comes forward and explains what transpired within the rundown tenement. He goes on to say that unfortunately his men were unable to stop the carnage, which resulted in the death of the so-called hostages. He lowers his head as if on cue and sheds a tear for the camera. On this note the reporter throws it back to the studio.

The anchorman in the studio tells the camera that Steel Pulse is being tried for crimes against humanity. He follows this up by giving a historical look back at why certain music was banned in the early 1990s. It seems that in the mid-1980s the American government held congressional meetings on the effects of rock and rap music on the country's children. This charge was led by Tipper Gore, which is why the law was called the Gore Act. At first, the American government stopped the production of heavy metal. Soon after this edict was passed into law, teams of Dragon Squads or musician hunters emerged around the country. To this day, many say that these people were formed and trained in secret camps financed by Jerry Falwell. Those who were caught were taken to special prisons where, it was rumored, bizarre and inhuman experiments took place to eradicate their minds of the devil music.

As with most fads, not unlike the Salem witch trials and the "Better Dead Than Red" experience of the 1950s, they targeted any type of music that preached free thought and independence from the American way. Well, it wasn't long until the movement spread to Canada, and then to England. After punk rock was wiped out and its musicians imprisoned, the parliamentary structure decided reggae was next to be eradicated. Many of its songs called for its listeners to rise up and revolt against society's ills. One song actually called for the destruction of Babylon, which was, as they understood it, the civilized world.

Up until this time, Steel Pulse had been the last reggae band still at large. To further infuriate the powers that be, they continued to play on the Musical Underground Railroad circuit.

Well, all that is over now.

The anchorman reaches up, grabs his ear and nods; he tells the audience that a verdict is about to be rendered on the Steel Pulse case. He then throws it back to the woman reporter.

The reporter explains to the audience that the professional jurors' deliberation lasted longer than any case in rent history. The total time was 10.57 seconds. They never even left the box; it was over so quickly. The pounding of the judge's gavel silences the reporter. As the courtroom quiets down, the judge looks at each of the defendants. Even though they stand before him locked in chains, they remain defiant. The judge stands up, points a finger at the Pulse and tells them that they have been deemed guilty by the court-appointed professional jury for inciting free thought and independence among the peoples of this world. He quotes directly from the words of Vice-President Tipper Gore: From this point forward no offensive and derogatory information, especially in musical form, shall be imposed on the peoples of the world. They will spend the rest of their natural lives in Hell's Paradise, a forbidding prison in the Falkland Islands. He goes on to say that in the good old days their crime would have warranted the death penalty. However, Hell's Paradise could be considered one step beyond death ... or a living hell on earth. On this note, he smiles and tells the Pulse to have a good life.

The journey to Hell's Paradise is a long and arduous one. As they ride in the prison barge their minds drift back to the days when their ancestors made a similar journey. The chains they bore take on a spiritual and musical quality. This interlude is broken when they arrive in hell. They are escorted off the ship and taken to the prison to be strip searched. After undergoing the degrading medical examinations they are taken to their cells. As their cell doors slam shut each man can feel his freedom slowly slip away.

After they've been caged for several days, the warden strolls in and tells the new inmates that it is his policy to talk to each new prisoner. For one thing, it adds to the family atmosphere he likes to promote among his inmates; more important, he at one time was a misguided musician himself so he understands their frame of mind. It is rumored that he is one of the few people to survive those early inhuman experiments in the late in the 1980s with no side effects ... or so they say.

Over the next several days the warden takes each man into his office for an intensive interrogation. Instead of getting the names and places of other musical cells, the warden gets to hear each man's philosophy on his music. Out of frustration, the warden puts each of the Pulse members in the hole: solitary confinement. They stay in the hole for two months. On the sixtieth day the warden goes down, expecting to watch the Pulse crawl out of their cells whimpering and crying like the musical scum they are. Instead, when the doors open all seven of the members stand tall, walk out and give a strange gesture to each other. The gesture is their way of telling themselves that they are all okay. Seeing this infuriates the warden so much that the knot in the back of his neck starts to throb. He storms off in a fiery rage.

Over the next several weeks, the tension in the prison increases as fight after fight breaks out. At first, the warden thinks nothing of it, but when seventy-five inmates start a riot in the courtyard, he knows something has to be done.

The members of Steel Pulse are summoned to the warden's office. He tells them that this prison is not unlike a plantation or slave ship in the good old days. When the natives got restless the slave master threw them a party. The slaves danced and sang until all the frustration they felt disappeared. It was like releasing a valve or, as the saying goes: "Music has charms to sooth a savage breast."

The warden proposes that they put on a concert. However, the music that they play must not excite the men. It must soothe them. They look at him with blank stares. He hands out a list of the top ten songs on the charts. The list includes four polkas, two Lawrence Welk songs, the muzzy version of "I Write the Songs" and "Ding-Dong! The Witch Is Dead" from *The Wizard of Oz*. The warden goes on to warn them not to try any funny stuff.

On the night of the concert, the whole prison turns out. Many inmates bring dates, some of whom are not too bad looking. The guards line the walls, ready to shoot at anything out of the ordinary.

The band walks up on the stage wearing chains on their wrists and ankles. Off to one side, the warden is watching from a private box. A hush falls over the crowd. Each band member takes his place on the stage. The lead singer looks at the sheet music and tears it up. The warden signals for a guard to shoot to kill. The guard fires a shot that lands at the feet of the singer. He slowly raises his chained arms, signaling his group to start playing.

The pure force of the bass line knocks the guards off the wall. The chains they wear simply drop off like paperweights. With this accomplished, they start to play like they never have before.

After a while, even the warden starts to sway to the pulsating sounds of the music.

A change seems to fall over the entire prison. People who were once mortal enemies are now enjoying the music side by side. Even though the war for music is far from over, the struggle continues ... by any means necessary.

Chapter 8
A Random Dream Thought ...

CELL BLOCK

INT. PRISON CELLS —DAY

The setting is a row of cells in a maximum-security prison. Inside each of the cells is a hardened criminal. In a voiceover we hear a judge sentencing each of them to their respective jail time. The camera dollies from cell to cell as the prisoners look directly into the lens. PRISONER #1, Asian, forties, male, stands in the first cell.

VO#1

You have been sentenced to two years in the state penitentiary for selling unlicensed firearms ...

Camera dollies to PRISONER #2, mid-twenties, black, female.

VO#2

Darlene Johnson, this court sentences you to spend three to six years in jail for one count of armed robbery and three counts of ...

Camera dollies to PRISONER # 3, sixteen years old, Hispanic, male.

VO#3

You stand before this court, showing no remorse for your crimes. With that in mind, I sentence you to be incarcerated for five to fifteen years for the drive-by shooting on ...

Camera dollies to cell #4 but no one is there. It searches the cell, and finally looks down. PRISONER #4, a five-year-old boy, dressed like a homeboy, stands there looking directly into the lens.

VO#4

In all my years on the bench I have never seen a more violent crime. The kidnapping and murder of a small store owner and his family is perhaps the most heinous of all crimes. For this felony you are to be sentenced to life imprisonment with no chance for parole. You, sir, will never hurt innocent people again.

FADE TO BLACK. INT. INSERT STAGE—DAY
We fade up on a .45 caliber handgun and a rattle sitting on a slow moving turntable. A childhood nursery-rhyme song can be heard in the background.

VO

There is one 'hood that most children never get to visit these days. It is a place that they are forced to leave at a time when they need it most.

(Sounds of typewriter keys.)
GRAPHIC: C - H - I - L - D - H - O - O - D

Chapter 9

DON'T MESS ...

"This is getting a little creepy."
—Wil

INTRODUCTION

The spark for this story comes from a summer when I was working on a concert series. I had gotten out a little early that day, and decided to see *Aliens* by James Cameron. What a movie! A lot of folks say that *Alien* by Ridley Scott is better. In my opinion, they are two completely different movies in two different genres. The first is a suspense drama, while the second is an action film, pure and simple. Both are the ultimate in adrenaline rushes.

Anyway, I remember coming out of the theatre and looking around. I was still jazzed from seeing the film and my mind was in overdrive. This happens to me when I see a movie, read a book or watch a television show that turns me on: I want to write something right then and there. Well, I looked down and saw my sneaker was untied. I stopped and tied it. When I looked up I saw a friend from college who was working in NYC whom I hadn't seen in a couple of months. We talked for a while about how things were going.

After he left, I remember thinking that if I hadn't stopped to tie my shoe, I would have missed him completely. How lucky was that? Or *was* it luck? Maybe it was fate. This got me thinking about fate and how it might work. I asked myself the "what if" question: "What if our lives are already scripted out in such a way that they are all interconnected?" I remember reading something about how a butterfly flapping its wings in China could affect the weather patterns in, say, Secaucus, New Jersey. The next question I asked myself was: "What if someone broke this pattern, either by mistake or on purpose, for his or her gain? Would the world fall apart? Would the earth spin off its axis and into the sun?" I didn't know the answer, but it got me thinking and writing.

"Don't Mess with Fate" was originally titled "Don't Fuck with Fate." I changed it not because of the word *fuck* but because the phrase "don't mess" seemed to sum up the idea better.

I remember when I finished writing it several folks said that the topic and what the lead character chooses to do was too edgy, or wasn't in good taste. I don't want to give away too much about the story, but I was told that it showed a black father in a bad light. At first I was pissed off at this statement because I thought: hell, it's just a story. Nothing deeper, nothing more. I have written several things that people find questionable. I love this. I learned a long time ago that a writer has to have a thick, thick skin to survive. Now, I'm not gonna sit here and tell you that I like people hating my material, but that comes with the territory. The most important thing is that you get a reaction, good or bad.

I can remember going on a screening tour of a short film entitled *The Session* I worked on, starring Butch Robinson, David Johnson and Eric Payne. The film was about a black militant group that kidnaps and deprograms a black yuppie (it was the '80s!). We screened the short and were answering questions from the audience. Several people told us that maybe we shouldn't be writing about these things. We should be writing about things that bring black folks together. One stood up and asked: "How come you had the character XB ["Extra-Black"] wearing a Malcolm X T-shirt?" He said that we should be more responsible. That was when I got mad. I remember telling them that I thought nothing was sacred and that I could write about anything I wanted to. Who's to decide what should be written about? The answer is: no one but the writer. I went on to say that if I had second thoughts about writing based what I thought people would think I wouldn't write anything. That's when my partner stood up and calmly explained to them that the film was a satire and the actors wore their own wardrobe because we couldn't afford a costume designer.

I will also say that some of my white friends have asked me: "What's with the black stuff? Your stories have more of a universal appeal; stick with that." My answer to them is that if they have to ask they'll never understand.

One time my father asked me if I was a writer who was black or if I was a black writer. I didn't have answer for him then, but now I'd have to say that I am both. I write therefore I am and every day in this country I am reminded that I am black.

I do have to say that I think my heritage, my background, and what I read and watch comes out in my writing. I decided a long time ago that I wanted to write stories that we as a people have not been in yet. Yes, there are times when race plays a role, but more often than not the people in my stories are three-dimensional characters, plain and simple.

Enough of this ... check out the story.

DON'T MESS ...

INT. WIL'S APT/LIVING ROOM—EVENING

The apartment looks like it's been to hell and back. Dirty clothes are scattered about the room. Half-full paper cups lie on their sides, spilling their contents onto the once-beige carpet. Month-old papers and magazines clutter the room. Food from Burger King, Mickey D's, Wendy's, Hardee's, Jimmy Jams Bar-BQ with the famous wizard sauce are piled up like a small mountain in the center of the room. Roaches and small rodents are having a field day picking over the leftovers. WIL DIAMOND, forty-five years old, black, six foot, leaps out of the darkness of a corner and swings his Louisville slugger at invisible enemies. The small apartment comes alive with the sounds of war. Helicopters hovering, soldiers yelling and guns firing fill the room with an unbearable noise.

WIL

Jonah ... Jonah! They're over-runnin' our position!
Fall back, goddamn it! Fall back!

Our Mr. Diamond is in the midst of a Vietnam flashback. They have plagued him since he returned to the world.

WIL

Please stop it!

The sounds slowly die down. Wil collapses in the center of the room, still holding the bat tightly. He is out of breath and a little dazed from his ordeal. There is a look in his eyes that would scare the ugly off an ape. His eyes seem to glow with intensity.

INT. LIMBO CURTAIN—?
On an insert stage stands ANNIE MAY "POO BUTT" DIAMOND, thirty-five years old, black. She was once was a fox and is now a heifer. She is the ex-wife of Wil. A graphic appears on the screen, explaining who she is. Her dialogue is spoken right into the camera, documentary style.

POO
Now? ... You want me to talk now? Okay, let's see, there's just so much to say about the man. Weeelll, Willy was never the same after the war. He ... he couldn't concentrate or anything. And when I mean anything, I mean everything, honey. Know what I'm talking 'bout? Ever since he came back he'd have these flashbacks. That's what the vet center called them. It scared the shit out of me. One time when we were sleeping he had a flashback and started to scream and jump around, like he was being attacked. Besides that, he was always mumbling weird shit like "Birds don't sing like that in the jungle," or "Poo," or *"Incoming!"*—weird, right? He was always coming up with these schemes. What schemes, you

ask? Oh, you one of those college boys, ain't ya? You know the kind ... ones that lead to quick money. One time he sank his whole veteran's check into coffins for pet rocks. I tried to tell him that pet rocks were dead. Know what he told me? That's what the coffins are for. It was like living with Ralph Kramden or something. Now tell me: do I look like Alice or what? All right, I'll calm down. Pins and needles, needles and pins, it's a happy woman who grins.

She grins, showing off all of her bright, white teeth.

POO (cont.)

Well, it was nonstop for years until the lottery came out. You can guess where all the money went then. You got that right. You know he wasn't like this at all before he went to Vietnam. He did get into a little trouble up in Motor City, but that was all behind him. When he came back he wasn't all there. I mean he wasn't all there physically. He was missing his leg from the knee down. The VA said that he were one of those robot things. He hated it when the kids in the neighborhood called him the bionic man or the six-cent man. He really didn't mean to hurt those kids but they taunted him to no end. And another thing ... hey, what time is it? No shit, *Love Connection* is on. I just love it when the black people are on.

INT. LIMBO CURTAIN—DAY

Effect to Lieutenant Colonel Willard "I'll find what you love most and kill it" Wilkerson, white, thirty-five years old, very Southern, with a long scar on his face, of the Third Battalion Recon Squad, Alpha company. He was Wil's commanding officer in 'Nam.

WILLARD

Hey boy, you got that thing running yet or what? Jesus Christ, I haven't waited this long for anything since Jesus was a pauper. Ready ? Good. What was the question? ... Oh yeah, ol' diamond in the rough was a piece of work. I remember when that boy landed in the bush. *Shiiit*, like most nig—Negroes of his persuasion he'd close his eyes when he fired the sixty millimeter. It's understandable, ya know. I think it's something to do with their brains. I remember back in the good old days the Klan wrote something on it. If my memory serves ... The coloreds only use one-tenth of their brain power. For if they did indeed use more they would have gotten the message that we, the all-powerful white man, didn't want them here. Am I still in? ... Like an idiot, I let my prescription lapse. Dues or something. Anyway, after a couple of firefights that boy never slept.

He stops to light a cigar.

It was spooky. When his dander was up, he was one mean sum' bitch. He'd be in a firefight all night long, nuking gooks left and right, then come morning he'd volunteer for an S and D that day. Shit, volunteering is somethin' only a nitwit would do; see, it's that brain thing in 'em. Something else: after all that fightin' and killin', he didn't get diddly-squat ... nada ... no promotion. Shit, after a nasty S and D mission he fell on those fucking punji sticks and lost his leg, he was no more good ... he lost his fire. And when you lose that, you're a dead man in 'Nam, bucko. A walking dead man. It's really too bad ... But then, his people are always getting what they deserve ... it's ... it's like it's their fate or something.

INT. LIMBO CURTAIN—?

Sammy is replaced by Danny Diamond, black, young, with a slight build. He is Wil's son.

DANNY

Daddy wasn't Daddy after he went away. He told me before he left that he was gonna do things he didn't like to people he didn't know and he couldn't tell me why. All he told me was that I wasn't old

117

enough to understand. Now I'm older and I still don't. When ... when he came back from Vietnam, he never played ball or anything. And when I say anything I mean everything. Daddy wasn't Daddy. I 'member one time I dropped a glass in the kitchen, and his eyes changed. He ... he called me gookee and other names I didn't understand. It took two policemans to hold him back. Daddy wasn't Daddy anymore. Do you know he left something over there in the war? He called it his little souvenir. I ... I think it was my fault 'cuz I asked him to bring me something back. He brought back this robot leg. But he couldn't run fast or anything. It wasn't like the bionic man at all. I ... I want my daddy back. Have you seen him?

INT. WIL'S APT/LIVING ROOM—EVENING

The phone rings, scaring the piss out of Wil. He swings his bat and watches as it cuts through the air with the greatest of ease. Perfect follow-through. Even Mr. October would have to smile at this mighty stroke. The phone explodes into a million pieces all over the slightly messy room. After it lands in a heap of plastic and wire on the floor, it keeps ringing. He continues to hit it, again and again, hoping to silence the electronic beast. He sits among the telephone wreckage he has wrought. The slugger slowly rolls out of his hands, into the trash. He sits with his head in his hands. He looks almost at peace, as if he has accomplished the one deed that would allow him to achieve self-actualization. The ringing continues to sound throughout the house. Dazed, he picks what is left of the receiver. The wires hang around his neck like a loose Texas necktie.

> WIL
> (dazed, softly)
>
> Hello ... hello.

He looks at the phone, questioning whether this indeed is reality or a continuation of his flashback. It is only after several moments that he realizes it is the kitchen extension that is ringing. He stumbles to his bare feet and slowly wanders over to the phone in the kitchen.

> WIL (OS)
>
> Hello ... yes, this is Wil Diamond.

Wil walks back into the living room and leans against the wall.

> WIL
>
> Yes, this is Wil Diamond. No, I'm not at the moment. Why? You're shitting me. Wait a minute here. Let me get this straight. You're going to give me two hundred bucks to clean up a house? One fu ... house? Of course I'll take it. When? Tomorrow? ... Don't wait for me, my man. I'm there yesterday.

He drops the phone to the floor and looks down. On the floor among everything else is the latest edition of the newspaper. The headline reads: 20 MILLION, WHO WILL WIN? Wil slides down the wall and picks it up and smiles.

INT. LIVING ROOM—DAY
Wil emerges from another room combing his hair. He walks over to his transistor radio and turns it on. As he readies himself for his big day the radio blasts the rap cut "Don't Mess with Fate."

WIL
(rubbing his hands together)
Wil, my bonny boy, this could be the big one. The one that gets my Poo back, and Danny too. What I'll do is buy two hundred dollars in lottery tickets, win and everything will be hunky dory ... and they say a black man can't make it in this country.

Wil scurries about the house like a man possessed, getting ready for his big day. Once he has finished doing what he has to do to make himself presentable, he stands in front of the broken mirror examining his reflection. His clothes seem clean and his face is shaved, save for the Band-Aid on his chin. If we could smell him he would indeed smell a wee bit better. He gives himself the high-five sign and moves toward the front door. As he departs he passes today's newspaper and picks it up.

WIL

All those willing to take a chance should get their
numbers in by eight p.m. tonight ... Sorry folks, I
think we have a winner.

Wil kisses the paper and does a little James Brown spin while
humming to the music. He grabs the doorknob and swings the
door open, letting in the bright sunlight.

WIL

Holy Jesus, holy Jesus, what a fucking great day!

He walks out into the light, a new man.

EXT. RESIDENTIAL STREET—DAY

Melody Lane is one of those Spielberg-type streets frequently
found in small-town America. Dads are cutting the grass and
kids are playing ball on the front lawn while moms gossip about
the latest affair between the high school physics teacher and a
twenty-year-old-looking sixteen-year-old sophomore. Wil walks
down the street, soaking it all in and loving it.

WIL

Will you look at this? What a neighborhood! Poo
would drop her load if she could fit her size nines in
the doorway of one of these cribs. I could put
Danny in one of those good white private schools
instead of that brick shithouse they call a school in

the city. This could be the start of something big.

Wil stops in front of 1869 Melody Lane. This house doesn't fit in on his dream street. It is old Victorian in style, falling apart, with grass as high as an elephant's eye.

WIL

Oh shit, I've got my work cut out for me here.
Daddy always said hard work was good for the soul.
Maybe that's why he's burning in hell right now ...

He spots a note pinned to the front door of the house. He walks up tentatively, knowing that he doesn't belong or fit in here. Before he grabs the note he looks around again, hoping no one is watching him. In one quick motion he grabs the note and holds it close to his body, protecting it for some unknown reason. He holds the note, turning it over in his hands, examining it. The paper isn't like anything he has felt before. He does remember seeing something like it in one of those sword-fighting movies he saw on television years ago. The writing on the envelope is medieval in style, as if it was written with a quill pen. It says: TO WHOM IT MAY CONCERN. Wil tears open the letter, slowly unfolds the note inside and reads it.

TO WHOM IT MAY CONCERN,

    YOU HAVE BEEN SENT OVER BY THE TEMP, INC. AGENCY TO CLEAN UP THE HOUSE, CUT THE GRASS, ETC. WHILE YOU ARE WORKING DO NOT

TALK OR BOTHER THE PERSON INSIDE. HE HAS
TOO MUCH WORK TO DO. IF YOU UNDERSTAND
THE ABOVE, PLEASE SIGN HERE._____
ENCLOSED IS THE MONEY WE AGREED UPON: $200
DOLLARS PLUS $50 DOLLARS FOR YOUR TROUBLE.

THANK YOU.
THE MANAGEMENT.

Wil looks at the note, a little confused.

                    WIL
    Hold on here. Mama didn't raise no retard. I'm not
    signing shit ...

Wil's eyes catch hold of the last sentence in the note. MONEY.
The big M word. As he unfolds the lower third of the note the
money falls out of it, floating to the porch. He grabs at it as it
falls, catching the currency.

                    WIL
    Well, well, well, this puts a whole 'nother light on
    this signing business. I guess it can't hurt, can it?

He pulls an ink-stained pen from his ink-stained shirt pocket
and writes his name on the paper. He holds the money in his
hand, looking at it, passing it from hand to hand as he counts
it. The note drops and is blown away, going to the place where

all lost paper goes.

                         WIL
    This is my lucky day. Boy, if Poo could only see her
    man now. All I got to do is get to a lottery place by
    eight and that twenty mil is as good as mine. Let's
    hit it.

Wil limps toward the garage; however, there is a bit of a skip in
his wobbly gait. Danny would be proud of his dad. He finds the
lawnmower and pulls the cable, starting it up.

EXT. FRONT YARD/HOUSE—DAY
Wil wipes his dirty hands on his already filthy jeans and looks
over his masterpiece. It has been transformed. He smiles. He
looks at the house and slowly starts to move toward it. He feels
good, almost proud of his morning's work. He looks at his
watch and sees that it is noon. As Wil turns toward the house
he remembers the note.

                         WIL
                   (thinks to himself)
    Don't talk ... Don't bother the person ... too busy ...

Wil shakes off this thought and half-leaps up the steps to the
porch. He knocks. Silence. Again he knocks. Again silence. He
slowly grabs the knob and turns. It opens. In order to fully open
it, he pushes it with all his might. It seems that the hinge has

been rusted shut from disuse.

INT. HOUSE—DAY
The sunlight that squeezes through the door reveals a cobweb-bed, dusty interior. Whirlpools of dust spin through the air as the wind from the outdoors finds it way inside. He steps inside, releasing the door. As it closes it takes the sunlight with it, shutting the interior in a glove of darkness. In total darkness Wil steps forward and trips on a step.

                         WIL
     Jesus Christ, I can't see a thing. It's as dark a virgin's
     pussy in here. Maybe that's why I don't do virgins
     anymore. If I could only find a light …

Out of the darkness, it comes. Light. A chandelier comes on, illuminating the entrance hall with strange and compelling shadows. But it is not the shadows that capture the full and undivided attention of our hero. It's the books: thousands upon thousands of books, lining both sides of the hallway.

                         WIL
     What the hell …

He walks over to a pile and sees that on the binder is a day, a year and a name: Wednesday, 2 BC/GORG.

WIL

Two BC ... what the hell is this? *The Flintstones*? I guess that makes me Barney Rubble ... Hey Bamm-Bamm!

Wil weaves his way through the walkway of words, looking into the many rooms. The candles cast eerie shadows on the walls, making his journey even stranger. In one room a cathedral-type structure built out of books has been erected. It looks like a shrine to something or someone.

WIL

At least the dude believes in a god of some kind.

The books he sees are diverse in size, shape and color. The only constant is the day, the year and a name written on the spines.

WIL

This is getting a little creepy. He must be one of those people who don't like to go outside or something, like I saw on *Oprah* the other day. Yeah, that must be it ...

His journey takes him through the maze of books. He looks at them in total disbelief. Every little noise in the house becomes alive with its own energy. Something other than disbelief begins to enter his mind and heart. Terror. Pure, unadulterated terror. The kind that has plagued humanity since the dawn of time.

Fear of the unknown. Wil looks around at his surroundings, not knowing what to do next. Being curious about the whole situation, he picks up one of the books and turns it over in his hands, feeling the weight of it. Just as he is about to open it a noise erupts through the darkness, scaring the bejesus out of him. He turns toward the source of the sound and sees a dim light coming from a doorway at the end of the hall. As he gets closer to the light, the sounds that surrounded him in 'Nam are slowly creeping into his reality. Wil is about to have one of his many flashbacks.

WIL

No, no, not now, please Lord …

They start as memories far, far away. He tries to make it down the hallway but as he gets closer and closer to the light, the sounds intensified to a deafening crescendo. The helicopter blades slicing through the air; muddy GI-issue army boots trudging through the rain-soaked rice paddies; M-16 and AK-47 fire cutting through the air, finding its way toward their unsuspecting targets; the pain-filled screams of his fallen comrades. All these are the sounds of war. Sounds so vivid they approach the physical state, taking on a life all their own. They can never be forgotten. Wil shakes his head, trying to clear the noises from his mind, hoping all the while that this is not his new reality. As he nears the door the sounds seem to be just around the corner.

WIL

Nnooo! Stop it, goddamn it, stop it!

INT. STUDY—DAY

Wil dives into the room, landing belly-first onto the dusty floor. Dust whirlpools into the air as he hits. He looks up through the dust to see a small figure sitting in a high chair that stands in front of a high desk. It reminds him of the kind of thing that Bob Cratchit sat on in *A Christmas Carol*.

WIL

Danny ... Danny, is that you, son?

As the dust settles his eyes focus on the figure in the chair. It is not his son. It is a small man dressed in a dark robe, wearing a pair of Ray-Ban shades. He proceeds to pick up a quill pen and write like a man possessed. Without missing a beat he picks up a huge eraser and begins to remove what is left of the page. He writes and erases like crazy in many of the books on his desk. Wil picks himself up and looks at the man with his mouth wide open. He finally finds his voice.

WIL

Hey, how ya' doin' ...?

Silence.

WIL

Could you point me toward the kitchen, so I can get
started? Oh yeah, I'm the guy the note was for. Oh
shit, I'm not supposed to talk to you. Sorry 'bout
that, man.

Silence. Wil clears his throat, trying to get the man's attention.
The man continues to work. Wil walks over to the gnome-like
character and waves his hand in front of the man's face. No response.

WIL

Look, I know you're busy like the note said, but all I
need to know is where the kitchen is ...

The little guy continues his work.

WIL

All right, I get the message. If you need a hand like
getting a book you can't reach or something, 'cuz
your so shor—busy and all, just let me know.

As if on cue, the guy leaps off the stool and walks over to a tall
stack of books. Still looking at the book in his hand, he lifts his
leg and, with a back kick, knocks a large book from the middle
of the pile onto his desk. Wil leaps forward, ready to catch the
stack of books if they fall. They don't.

WIL

Hey look, I'm sorry if ...

He is talking to an empty space. The little person is gone.

WIL

What the hell ...?

Before he can finish his sentence the strange, acrobatic man reenters the room through Wil's legs. Wil screams and grabs his nuts.

WIL

Hey! I don't play that gay shit!

The man resumes his work at his desk.

WIL

Yo! I'm talking to you!

Ignoring him, the little person picks up another book and thumbs through it. Wil watches him, totally confused. He throws up his hands.

WIL

Oh, forget it. Where the hell is that kitchen?

He leaves.

INT. KITCHEN/HOUSE—DAY

Wil finishes the dishes and ties up a garbage bag. He glances at his watch and notices that his watch has stopped at 12:03 p.m. He bangs on the crystal, getting no response from the timepiece whatsoever.

                    WIL
    I knew I shouldn't have gotten this watch off the
    street.

He opens the back door and ...

EXT. BACK YARD/HOUSE—DAY

... goes out into the backyard. Wil's knees buckle as he almost falls to the ground.

                    WIL
    What the hell is going on now?

Wil grabs his head, trying to push out the pain. He glances at his watch and sees that the hands are spinning around as if trying to catch up to the present time. It is as if time were catching up with itself. His watch stops at 2:12 p.m.

                    WIL
    Jesus, I must have had a relapse or something.
    Thank God there's still plenty of time to get my
    ticket in.

He tries to shake off the effect and slowly walks over to the trash can to dump the garbage bag he is carrying. He is still a little confused, but returns to the house. The back door is locked so he has to enter the house through the front door.

INT. MAIN ENTRANCE/HOUSE—DAY
Wil walks in the front door wiping his dirty hands on his dirty jeans, making them anything but clean. He looks at the cobwebs that hang all over the house.

                    WIL
Maybe I should try to clean off some of these spider-webs.

He looks around the main room examining the cobwebs in their own surroundings. They seem to belong here. He takes a rag out of his back pocket and starts to dust. The room soon becomes one big dust cloud. Wil coughs and almost hacks up a lung.

INT. MAIN ENTRANCE/HOUSE—DAY
Wil stands up holding a bucket and sponge and looks at his work. It looks exactly the same.

                    WIL
This place is gonna need more than elbow grease.

Wil exits and comes back without the bucket and sponge.

WIL

I think I've earned the money they paid me. Let me
just get the hell out of this funhouse. It's been giving
me the willies all day long.

He backs up the couple of steps that gave him so much trouble
coming into the house. As he moves, he never takes his eyes off
the light emanating from the end of the hall.

WIL

Yo, little man, I'm outta here. Look, it's been real ...
[under his breath] real fucking strange.

He looks down the hall. Nothing. No response.

WIL

What was that? Oh no, you don't have to thank me.
It was my pleasure. Did I tell you that I'm gonna
win the lottery with this money?

Silence. He looks at his watch to check the time and sees that
the hands are stuck at 2:13 p.m. He taps on the face, trying to
get it to work. It doesn't. Wil shrugs, turns and grabs the doorknob. As he opens the door, the sunlight once again invades the
other reality. Wil feels the dizziness that hit him before and
grabs the door for support. He glances down at his watch to see
the hands spin around, till they stop at 4:25 p.m. He does a
double-take and is about to walk out into the madness he calls

reality when he stops and takes out his money and counts it again. He looks as if he were making a major decision. He steps back in and lets the door close, once again shutting him in with all the books and the small man. The darkness engulfs him. After several moments the chandelier sparks to life.

                              WIL
    I know that I'm gonna win this lottery, but you
    never can tell ... I wonder if I can arrange to come
    back here on a regular basis. It's not hard work—it's
    kinda creepy, in fact—but a paycheck's a paycheck.

He slowly moves down the hall, toward the light of the study that burns through the darkness.

INT. STUDY/HOUSE—DAY
He finally reaches it, only to be greeted by an empty room.

                              WIL
    Look, little man, I've done my best to ...

Standing in the doorway, he looks around the room, seeing nothing but the books that inhabit this inner sanctum. The candles by the desk go out by themselves, casting the room into the now-familiar darkness. Wil is scared shitless.

                              WIL
    Oh shit!

Wil screams in the darkness. Something or someone has entered the room. A match is struck, exploding into a yellowish-white light. The little guy's face comes into the light, bringing the already scared Wil to new heights of terror. The man touches the match to the wick of another candle. The room comes to life once again.

WIL

Damn!... Cut it out, all right?

The little man resumes writing and erasing in his mysterious books.

WIL

Look, I'm sorry for bothering you like this—and I remember the note and everything—but I just have one question that I wanted to ask you.

The man continues to work.

WIL

I know I said some stupid shit before, but I'm willing to let bygones be bygones. Anyway, I'm wondering if I could come by, say, twice a month to clean up, you know?

No response.

WIL

Sir? ... Ah, pardon ...

The strange man leaps down, quickly crosses the floor and runs through Wil's legs, out the door and out of sight. Wil grabs his nuts and turns to see where he went.

WIL

I'm really starting to hate this shit.

He turns back and looks around the room. His eye is drawn to the candle on the desk. He walks over and picks up the book his little friend has been writing in. Looking at the spine of the book, he sees the date: July 9, 1760/Jaminson. Wil opens the book to where he was working and sees on top of the page, written in a medieval scrawl, a name, Burford Samuelson Jaminson, followed by a list.

BURFORD SAMUELSON JAMINSON
I. BORN JULY 9, 1760. LONDON, ENGLAND.
II. AUGUST 20, 1767. LOSES LEFT EYE IN CARRIAGE ACCIDENT.
III. JANUARY 8, 1773. GOES TO THE COLONIES AND JOINS GENERAL WASHINGTON'S FORCES.
IV. MAY 10, 1780. MARRIES BETTY JO IBSEN.
V. AUGUST 11, 1785. ACCIDENTLY KILLS WIFE IN ARGUMENT.
VI. AUGUST 12, 1785. GOES WEST WITH EXPEDI-

TION AND IS ATTACKED BY BEAR. LOSES MOVE-
MENT IN RIGHT HAND.

VII. OCTOBER 30, 1787. OPENS STORE IN NORTH-
WEST TERRITORIES. VERY SUCCESSFUL.

VIII. MARCH 18, 1795. REMARRIES. WIFE IS A
COUSIN. ALL FOUR KIDS AFFECTED.

IX. APRIL 22, 1800. LEAVES ON SHIP FOR THE ORI-
ENT.

X. SEPTEMBER 5, 1801.
DIES. SHIP LOST AT SEA.

Wil looks up from the paper, totally confused.

WIL

Wait a minute ... the shrimp writes this stuff? What
is this, the *Twilight Zone* or something? This little
guy is tripping. No wonder they keep him in this
house.

Wil starts to pace the room, back and forth, back and forth.

WIL

Wake up, Willy. I can't believe for a second that he
writes this stuff and it comes true. No way, no way
... they'd put me in the loony bin if they thought I
believed this shit ... But maybe I should just check it
out ...

Wil continues to pace around the room, He suddenly stops and snaps his fingers.

                              WIL
        I got it! September 9, 1950 ...

Wil searches the room, looking for something. He is careful with the books as he examines them so as not to leave a clue that he was looking at them.

INT. HOUSE/MONTAGE—DAY

Wil's search for his proof takes him throughout the house. At this point he has all but forgotten the master of the house and has become consumed with finding the proof. He looks through what seems hundreds and hundreds of books before he finds what he looking for. He finally holds up his prize, gazing at the title. September 9, 1950/Washington. He looks for a place to sit and examine the book. Wil winds up in the cathedral room and closes the door.

INT. HOUSE/CATHEDRAL ROOM—DAY

He walks in, thumbing his way through the book.

                              WIL
        Thank God they're in some kind of order, else I
        would have never found it. Let's see ... J ... J ...

He sits down in front of the shrine and continues to look

through the book. At last he finds it: Jonah Washington.

JONAH WASHINGTON
I. SEPTEMBER 9, 1950. RALEIGH, NORTH CAROLINA.
II. JANUARY 10, 1962. LOSES VIRGINITY TO LU ANN
PICKER IN BARN.
III. OCTOBER 13, 1966. DROPS OUT OF HIGH
SCHOOL. EXTENT OF EDUCATION.
IV. SEPTEMBER 22, 1968. DRAFTED VIETNAM WAR.
V. JUNE 10, 1969. RAPES AND KILLS VIETNAM FAM-
ILY AFTER SEARCH-AND-DESTROY MISSION.
VI. JUNE 11, 1969. CAPTURED BY VIETCONG. TAKEN
TO PRISON CAMP. TORTURED.
VII. SEPTEMBER 21, 1969. ESCAPE ATTEMPT FAILS.
VIII. MARCH 2, 1970. FORCED TO CONFESS.
IX. MAY 13, 1970. GETS MALARIA.
X. AUGUST 1, 1970. DIES. COMMITS SUICIDE BY
HANGING HIMSELF WITH A TOWEL.

Wil is reduced to tears.

WIL

Jesus Christ! Not that—anything but that. He was
the best. I ... I always wondered what happened to
him after that S and D mission in that village. I lost
my leg and he winds up taking his life.

Wil rests his head in his hands and takes a moment.

WIL

Shit, it's true, I can't believe it. The guy writes people's fates. A fucking little— Who is gonna believe this?

Wil stops in his thoughts and realizes something.

INT. HOUSE—DAY

Once again he runs through the house, looking for the answer to his problems. After a while he happens upon what he is looking for. It looks like all the others, no different. No different at all. His trembling hand reaches out and grabs it. December 25, 1949/Diamond. He carries the book, clutched to his breast as if to hide it from the world. He goes back to the little man's cathedral room.

INT. HOUSE/CATHEDRAL—EVENING

He sits at the desk and flips through the pages. Names pass his eyes, making no connection with his brain. He is looking for something in particular. His own destiny.

WIL

William Christian Diamond.

He closes his eyes.

WIL

Should I? It's almost blasphemous.

He opens his eyes and reads his fate.

WILLIAM CHRISTIAN DIAMOND*
I. DECEMBER 25, 1945. BORN. SHOWEM, ALABAMA.
II. JUNE 5, 1950. MOLESTED BY OLDER UNCLE.
III. APRIL 1, 1957. LOSES VIRGINITY TO ANNE MAY JOHNSON.
IV. MARCH 3, 1962. MOVES TO DETROIT, MICHIGAN.
V. JULY 6, 1964. JOINS BLACK PANTHER MOVEMENT.
VI. AUGUST 20, 1964. INVOLVED IN ALTERCATION WITH DETROIT POLICE, KILLING ONE. HE MOVES BACK TO SHOWEM, ALABAMA.
VII. OCTOBER 5, 1964. MARRIES ANNE MAY JOHNSON.
VIII. NOVEMBER 10, 1965. DRAFTED INTO THE VIETNAM WAR.
IX. SEPTEMBER 11, 2010. ACCIDENTLY KILLS SON.
X. FEBRUARY 6, 2020. WINS LOTTERY FOR 70 MILLION DOLLARS.
*HAVE TO REWORK SCHEDULE. FORGOT TO PUT IN WHEN HE DIES.

Wil can't believe his eyes. His breathing deepens as he tries to comprehend what he has just read.

WIL
The lottery! The motherfuckin' lottery! I can't be-

141

lieve it! After all these years. I knew it would happen, I just knew it. Everybody said it wouldn't, but here it is in black and white. Wait till Poo hears this. She'll be all over me like ugly on an ape. Yeah, she'll come running, and Danny will look up to me again.

Wil turns when he hears a noise out in the hall.

WIL

Who's there? Hey, if that's you, I'm sorry ...Out of the darkness walk Poo and Danny, hand in hand.

POO

We are all so proud of you, Willy. Aren't we, Danny?

Danny looks up at his mother and then runs toward his father. He runs several steps and jumps into his arms. Wil reaches out to catch him. Danny disappears into nothing. Wil grabs at thin air. All the joy washes from his face as he remembers the ninth line in his fate list.

POO

That's right, Willy ... Danny won't be with us by the time you win the lottery. Remember, Willy, you can never get something for nothing.

Poo fades into the background.

WIL

Wait, Poo! You don't understand ... I could never
hurt Danny. I love him. I really do. He's my son too.
He is a little clumsy sometimes. I remember that
time in the kitchen. I couldn't kill him. It ... said it
was an accident, right here, see.

He holds up the book. He is alone.

WIL

I'm sure I didn't mean to.

Wil sits down on the floor with his head in his hands. He
slowly draws circles in the dust that covers the floor.

WIL

The money. It's all I ever wanted. To win something. I've always been a loser. In marriage ... in
'Nam... in fatherhood ... and now in my own fate.
In order to win the lottery I have to kill my son. It
says it's an accident, I couldn't do that, not to
Danny. Jesus Christ, why can't Wil Diamond win
for once. My son ... my son ... the lottery ...

His mind drifts. The shadows of the house seem to take on a
life all their own. Out of one of them walks Lt. Col. Willard
Wilkerson.

WILLARD

Hey, boy! What's it gonna be? The money or the
burrhead? Come on, there are enough of you in the
world anyway. One less ain't gonna matter none.
Go for the bucks, you buck you.

Wil sits up in shock as he listens to his CO.

WILLARD
(sings)

Buck, buck, go for the bucks ... buck, buck, go for
the bucks ...

Wil turns from the colonel and covers his ears.

WIL

Stop it ... stop it!

The singing stops. He looks up to see Poo standing next to
Willard.

POO

So we meet again. Tell me, do we remember what I
told you last time we spoke?

Wil just stares at her.

POO

What's a matter, cat got that wild-ass tongue of yours? Let's take a look at your life so far, shall we? You've killed people ... alienated your son ... shit on me ... In the future you'll kill your son ... and win seventy million dollars.

Willard steps in and puts a knife to Poo's throat. She doesn't struggle.

WILLARD

Don't listen to her. You know money can buy your way out of your color. It's not your fault you're colored. Do yourself a favor and use the money with a clean conscience and forget about the pickaninny. Shit, the way you people fuck ...

Danny materializes into the room and kicks Willard in the shin. He lets go of Poo, who spins around and kicks him in the balls. He doubles over. Danny stares at his father.

DANNY

Daddy, I didn't mean to drop that glass. I'm sorry. I'm sorry too that I made you bring back your robot leg. You said I didn't understand and you were right. I don't understand why you don't call anymore. Why, Daddy, why?

All three people start talking at once. Wil grabs his ears and closes his eyes.

WIL

Nnooo!

The voices and the people disappear as Wil's screams echo through the room. Wil falls to his knees once again.

WIL

Will you shut the hell up! Leave me alone! Why don't you let me make up your own mind for once? That would be a first, wouldn't it, Poo? All my damned life people have told me what to do. My parents ... the Panthers ... my nagging wife... the army ... and now a short motherfucker! Well, it stops right now! No more, no more! For once, I'll make up my own mind. My own. Does everybody hear that? I said: Do ... you ... hear... me?

Wil looks around the room for an answer. He gets none.

WIL
(out of breath)
My own mind ... my own mind. Jesus, this shit is driving me crazy. Calm down. Don't blow it now.

He takes a deep breath.

WIL

Whew ... let's see, the army did teach me to analyze the situation and devise a tactical plan of attack. If we look at this thing logically, I can see that there are both good and bad points. We have a boatload of money on one hand, and on the other there is the death of my son—killed accidentally according to the list. Poo is still very bad in the kid department, so another kid is not out of the question. But on the other hand the money is still too far away to enjoy it. I figure that I'll be close to seventy-five years old when the year 2020 rolls around. The age problem is the thing here. There's got to be a way to speed things up a bit. Think ... think ...

He paces the room, thinking like he has never done before.

WIL (cont.)

What ... if ...I ... were ... to ... kill ... my ... son... say tomorrow, instead of waiting till 1998—maybe I'll get the money two years from now. Yeah, maybe that's how it works. I'm sorry, Danny, it's for the best.

Wil stands up again and enters the hallway.

INT. HOUSE/MAIN ENTRANCE—DAY

He looks around the entrance hall and slowly begins to make

his way toward the door through the maze of books. Once there, he puts his hand on the knob and tries to turn it. It won't turn. He tries again. Nothing. A panic begins to rise, first through his veins, then through his muscles, forcing its way to his eyes. They reflect something Wil has felt before. Not physical terror but terror of the mind. He overcomes this feeling and reaches out and grabs the knob with two hands. He tries to turn the knob with all his might. It snaps off in his hands. He looks at the knob as if he has never seen one before.

VOICE (OS)

It won't work, Wil.

Wil turns to see the man standing about twenty yards away. He is wearing the same robe and glasses as before. He takes several steps toward Wil, who throws himself up against the door.

DESTINY

(in Poo's voice)

What's a matter, Wil, cat got that wild-ass tongue of yours?

Wil looks on in terror as the little guy giggles to himself.

DESTINY

Sorry about that, Mr. Diamond. But I couldn't resist. Say, is it all right if I call you Wil?

WIL

What ... who the hell are you?

DESTINY

Pardon my rudeness. My name is I. M. Destiny, sir.

Destiny bows to his visitor.

DESTINY

And you are William Christian Diamond. A man
who wishes to change his fate.

WIL

What the hell are you talking about ...change my ...
uh, fate.

DESTINY

You plan to kill your son tomorrow instead of waiting for fate to runs its course.

WIL

How do you know that?

DESTINY

Wil, I am the one who wrote your fate, as well as
well as the fates of those in the past, present and
future. This house has been placed in between time
so that I may constantly update everyone's fate. I'm
not sure how it all works, but it does. I was chosen
to do this a very long time ago. I'm just a cog in the
big machine. Everything has been worked out per-
fectly.

WIL

What does all this have to do with me?

DESTINY

Everyone's fate is connected, Wil. Everything and everyone is interrelated. Have you ever been walking down the street and stopped to tie your shoe for a second, and when you looked up there was someone you hadn't seen in years? Well, I write that stuff—it's me. The clothes you put on, which foot you step with first determine not only your fate but everyone else's too.

WIL

All I want is what's mine. All my life I've been a loser, and here I have a chance ... one chance in seventy million. I just want it now, and I must be right about changing my fate, 'cuz if I was wrong, you wouldn't be here trying to stop me.

Destiny takes several steps back as if he's been hit with a ton of bricks.

DESTINY

You don't understand ... now that you know that your son will be accidentally killed by your hand, why not use the next twenty years to reestablish your relationship and reach a peace with yourself?

Wil leaps forward to make a point.

WIL

Peace! That's something I've never known and never will. Now money is something different—it can help you buy your way into a whole lot of things. I'm not sure that peace of mind is one of them, but I'm willing to take that chance.

DESTINY

This chance you speak of will mess up everything. You have to understand that—you can't change fate. It changes you. It just is. Live with that fact.

WIL

But it said I'll win. You wrote it. I just want it a little early, that's all.

DESTINY

I'm sorry, Wil. That's the way it goes.

WIL

I've had enough of this shit. Let me out of here before I go off.

DESTINY
(laughs)

Go off ... go off ... oh, that infamous temper of yours. Isn't that the thing that got you in trouble in Detroit?

Wil steps toward Destiny.

DESTINY

That shit don't play here, Willy. Don't forget that I

wrote your life. That means I know what you're going to do before you even think about doing it. Besides, if I let you go and change your fate, I'd have to rewrite all these motherfucking books, and I'm not about to do that for anyone.

Wil screams and rushes Destiny. Destiny doesn't give any ground. All he does is reach out his arm. Wil stops hard when he hits Destiny's hand. He screams in pain as he grabs the hand. Destiny closes the hand that touches Wil's chest. Wil lets out a bloodcurdling scream and drops to the floor. Destiny stands in the middle of the floor with Wil's heart in his hand. It beats twice and dies. He looks at the organ and drops it. It lies there. Destiny collapses in a heap and cries.

DESTINY

You see, Wil, you don't mess with fate. You just don't mess ...

INT. ANOTHER HOUSE—DAY

In another land far, far away there stands a house. It is not unlike I. M. Destiny's. The interior is filled with books. A very old man sits at a high desk. He looks up as if he hears Destiny shedding tears.

OLD MAN

Oh *nnnooo!* What the hell has happened?

He shuts his eyes tightly as if to see the problem in his mind. Tears fall down his wrinkled face.

OLD MAN

Destiny, how could you do it? Everything's ruined. You weren't supposed to kill him. I didn't write it that way. I told them it'd be a problem. But would they listen? Oh no! Oh jeez, it took thousands of years to plan it all out.

He pounds on the desk in frustration.

OLD MAN

Wait a minute. There just may be a chance... a chance that Destiny's blunder didn't upset the fate line. Maybe it isn't in a direct relationship with what we have been working toward all these years.

The old man pulls out a slide rule and protractor and makes a series of calculations. After several minutes he stops.

OLD MAN

It too close to tell. I've got to find Destiny's entries for the blessed event.

He gets up and slowly looks through the stacks of books. Each one has a name at the top.

OLD MAN

Ah, here's Destiny's book. Out of all of my fate
writers, I never thought he would mess up like this
... He was one of my best students. Maybe it isn't all
that bad ... Let's see.

He looks through the many pages at hyper-speed and stops at
the name Mary Kay Belter. He traces his finger down the list
and stops at the fifth entry. He sighs and pulls out a huge eraser
and begins to erase the list from the bottom. His hand moves
allowing us to see the fifth entry:

V. DECEMBER 25, 5025. GIVES BIRTH TO THE MES-
SIAH.

OLD MAN

Why did he do it? He had to know we would have
to start all over again. All the planning down the
drain ...

He cries, knowing the amount of work that has to be redone.

Chapter 10
A Random Dream Thought ...

HUNTING

INT. '50S STYLE DEN/B&W—DAY
A den that looks like something out of the *Father Knows Best* series. Like the series, it is shot in black and white. It is filled with a boatload of books. A fire rages in the fireplace and the walls are covered with numerous stuffed animal heads. Out steps a man who resembles Bing Crosby, pipe and all. He is decked out in hunting apparel, right down to the shotgun he is carrying.

HUNTER

Hunting is a way of life. And if you're like me—and
I know you are—you know that there is nothing
like the feel of a hand-crafted weapon ...

He strokes his weapon lovingly.

EXT. ALLEY/COLOR—NIGHT
In the shadows a hand pulls a handgun from the waistband of a

pair of jeans. The gun is turned over and over.

INT. '50S STYLE DEN/B&W—DAY

The hunter stands up from petting his Irish setter and looks into the camera.

> HUNTER
>
> One of the most important rules to remember when hunting is to use the correct ammunition. If you need assistance in choosing, please contact your closest gun dealer ...

EXT. ALLEY/COLOR—NIGHT

In one quick motion, a clip is shoved into the gun and it is cocked, placing a bullet in the chamber.

INT. '50S STYLE DEN/B&W—DAY

His hand rests on one of the animal heads.

> HUNTER
>
> After locating your prey, try to use your environment as a source of cover ...

EXT. ALLEY/COLOR—NIGHT

In the shadows the glowing end of a cigarette can be seen. From his POV we see that he scans the surroundings looking for his mark. Several people walk by him: an old man, several young women, a little boy and several homeboys.

HUNTER (OC)

Choosing your prey can be a very important decision. The very old and very young animals will not
yield the meat every hunter searches for. So wait for
your target. Be patient.

The mugger sees a man finishing up his business with an auto-
matic teller machine. The man quickly puts his money in his
wallet and walks away.

HUNTER (OC)

Once you have him in your sights, stalk him. Not
too close—you don't want to scare him. Have your
weapon at the ready.

The mugger pulls his gun out as he closes in.

INT. '50s STYLE DEN/B&W—DAY
He is pointing his shotgun directly at the camera.

HUNTER

Now comes that all-important moment when it's
just you and your gun against nature. If you follow
these simple rules, you will join the thousands of
people who enjoy hunting on a regular basis.

EXT. STREET/COLOR—NIGHT
From the mugger's POV, we see him run up to his prey. The

man turns and tries to run. The mugger chases him into an alley, cornering him. The mugger raises his gun and closes in. The scene freezes on the agonized face of the man.

HUNTER (OC)
And remember, a good hunter is a smart hunter. So come on. Grab your gun, put on those fatigues, and enter the world of the successful hunter.

Fade to black. A gunshot is heard.

Chapter 11

RUNNING

"(Whisper)"
—Paul

INTRODUCTION

I have always been a sucker for movies or stories that hit you right in the gut. You know, the ones that leave a lump in your throat. To name a few: *Brian's Song, West Side Story, Oliver!* (the last act), *Cooley High* and *The Dead Zone*. I decided that I wanted to write a story that affected people like the movies above. Let me just say that this not an easy thing to do. It took me a while, but I finally penned the following short story. It may not affect you as it did me, but it satisfied my desire to generate a story in this genre.

I got the idea one night after some friends and I were playing ball late one night in a quiet park in Weehawken, NJ. Five-O rolled up on us and said that the park was closed for the evening and we had to leave. We made some noise about how we weren't hurting anyone, but they insisted. We rolled out in a friend's car. We had played hard that night and decided to get some brews. As we drove, we noticed the gumballs in the rear-view mirror. We pulled over and had to endure them searching our trunk and questioning us for no reason at all. Let me say that I have friends who are in law enforcement, but I follow Richard Pryor's advice when dealing with them. On his *Is It Something I Said?* album he says that when the police approach a black man it is important to say exactly what you are doing: "I am now getting out of my car ... I am now handing you my license."

The other thing that helped spark this idea was that I was running every day. It really helped me clear my mind when I had something to figure out. Your mind seems to leave your body as your legs pound the pavement. I thought then and still think that this is a perfect time to Dream Think. The character in this story achieves his dream thought or answer to a difficult problem while running. Maybe you will too ...

RUNNING

Pick a city, any city in these United States ... no, scratch that—throughout the whole world—whose news of the day isn't filled with racism, death or sadness. It isn't possible in this day and age. However, there is a man trying just to do that. He sits in his living room watching his Sony Trinitron TV, listening to his all-news-searching Panasonic radio, which sits within his Technic component stereo system. He reads twenty or so newspapers searching for some type of answer, some glimmer of hope that would stop him from doing what he is planning.

Over several days, which soon turn into weeks; we watch him scan these information sources for the clue in question. Soon it becomes apparent that he may not know what he is looking for. This fact does not deter him from searching for it. Whatever it is. As he sits there in his one-bedroom apartment on the Upper-Upper West Side his phone rings continually, almost like clockwork. Toward the beginning of his quest the messages were as follows:

10 a.m. Mr. Smithers, his boss at the computer firm, asking if he is coming in to work today. They need him to finish designing the software for the Spectrum Project.

Noon. Susan Wilkerson, his lady of one and a half years, calls to ask what happened to him last night. He really missed a happening thing at B Smiths, and B herself was asking about him.

4 p.m. Jaime Sperry, his boy on the job, calls to ask what the fuck is going on. Smithers is starting to get pissed.

Several days later:

9:02 a.m. Smithers tells him that he'd better call ASAP, or else. The Spectrum people are getting nervous. Is it more money ... is that it? We can talk about that too.

10:15, 12:15 Susan asks him what the hell is going on: Did I do something wrong? Was it that I called you lazy for not being happy on your job? I'm kind of sorry about that.

12:23 p.m. Jaime: Look, man, I don't know what's going on but you're making yourself look bad in front of Smithers. I'm trying to cover for you. By the way, where are your notes on the Spectrum Project? Just curious. Hang in there, buddy.

Several days later:

10:05 a.m. Boss: Sperry told me that you used to have a drug problem. It wasn't crack, was it? In fact, he went on to say that that was the reason you were fired from your last job. Is that true, Williams? Oh, by the way he's taken over the Spectrum account for you. He's a good man. I'm glad you recommended him for a job. At least you did something right. This is the last message I'm going to leave, Williams. *Click!*

1:15 p.m. Jamie: Look, man, I didn't know that I was going to get the account. It just happened ... Oh yeah, that drug thing just slipped out. Sorry about that, pal. You know us brothers have to stick together. By the way, where are your notes on the financial analysis concerning the fourth-quarter profits for the account? Call me.

4:15 p.m. Susan: Look, motherfucker, I'm tired of making excuses for your ass. Oh, and I found a new man and he's rich, too.

Paul doesn't pay any attention to these messages. He just keeps searching. After another week of this he gets a call from someone he does want to talk to: his grandfather.

"Well, son, I'm not sure I understand what you mean, but it sounds important to you. And if it's important to you it's important to me. Is there anything that I can do to help? ... Sure, I'll call your mother ... What else ? ... Yeah ... Let me get a pen ... all right, got one ... Hmm ... and who should I say this to? ... The press? You sure you all right, son? ... Okay, okay, I believe you. When should I do this? Two weeks from today? You take care of yourself. I love you too.

The phone disconnects.

Paul stands there holding the phone in his hands. His eyes are squeezed shut. He appears to be praying. When he finishes, he slowly opens his eyes, allowing a lone tear to fall down his face. He takes a deep breath and replaces the phone, silencing the annoying phone-off-the-hook sound.

Slowly, deliberately, he goes around his small apartment and shuts off his electronic news-gathering system. He straightens up his home, putting all his papers in a neat pile, throwing away all the delivery food containers and washing the many dishes that have piled up over the last week. Upon finishing these tasks, he removes his soiled clothing and runs a steaming-hot shower. As the steam cloud builds in the bathroom, his image in the mirror slowly disappears from view.

After washing up, he reappears in his small living room dripping wet from his shower. He walks over to the sofa where he has laid out his running gear. He slowly puts on his jockstrap and a pair of good running socks. He pulls on a pair of shorts, then a pair of well-worn sweatpants. On top he wears a T-shirt and a matching zip-up, lightweight jogging jacket. His armor in place, he takes a deep breath and starts to limber up. He slowly stretches every muscle in his body to the point where he feels that he is ready to go. He walks out of the door, never to return again.

He opens the front door of his building, letting himself out into the brisk fall breeze. He looks around and surveys his surroundings, which he has called home for the last eight years of his life. To his right he sees a homeless person huddled in the corner of the building. Paul starts to smile as he sees several well-dressed executives approach the man. One of the men holds out a twenty-dollar bill to the old man. Tentatively, he reaches out to take it. The well-dressed man quickly pulls it away, allowing the old man's hand to close around nothing but air.

"You people have to learn that money is something to be earned and not to be given away. Just looking at you makes me ill. You smell like shit and look like it too," he says with disdain.

The old man starts to cry in a mumbling manner, which triggers snickers from the businessmen. "What a waste product," the businessman says over his shoulder as he and his friend walk away.

Paul walks over to the crying homeless man and smiles. The man looks up into Paul's eyes and sees something he has never seen in someone's eyes before: the truth. Soon he starts to smile back at Paul. The two strangers shake hands warmly. Paul turns and starts to jog down the street southward, toward the George Washington Bridge.

We catch up with our runner two weeks later. By this time he is somewhere south of Washington, D.C. Paul's pace is strong and steady, but measured. He is in no hurry. In his mind he puts off all thoughts of hunger, even though the pang is getting stronger with each step. Out of nowhere a television-news microwave truck pulls up beside him. In the opening of the side door sit a female reporter and a cameraman holding a D-Betacam unit. Standing above the reporter is a soundman extending a fish pole with a shotgun microphone attached to the end.

"So tell me, Mr. Williams, why are you doing this ... this thing? Your grandfather—Samuel Williams, I believe—called the UPI wire service and told a tale of his grandson trying to stop racism by running. Is that true?" she yells out through the side entrance of the van. Before Paul can answer, another news van pulls up with a similar setup. It almost hits its rival in the side; almost spills its contents out into the road.

"Tell me, Mr. Williams, how will running stop racism all over the world? By bringing attention to it? That's not a bad angle, I grant you, but it won't work. Tell me—" The reporter's sentence is cut off when the other news van rams hers from behind. Soon the news vans are jousting with each other, using the fish poles to whack each other senseless. They drive off, forgetting about Paul and his now public cause.

The next week and a half are a whirlwind. Paul has become a media sensation. *Time*, *Life* and *People* magazines have done covers on him, *ET* has done an in-depth weeklong series on what elements in his life could have caused him to pursue this lofty goal. For one week Paul's face is everywhere and on everything. His former boss, best friend and girlfriend have all claimed responsibility for giving him the inspiration for running against racism. (A side note: Jaime and Susan used their interview on *ET* to announce their upcoming marriage that will be held at B Smith's.)

People drive around looking for Paul to wish him luck and give him food and support. Mayor Dinkins has proclaimed Paul Williams Day in New York City. All this adulation lasts one week to the day. It stops because of the arrival of Lady Diana. This doesn't bother Paul one bit; in fact, he is relieved to be left alone.

He continues to run. South.

Paul's travels take him to the outskirts of Georgia. He feels good today, even though his running shoes are all but falling off his feet. He is only a shadow of his former self as he runs down the road. Behind him he hears a car horn blaring. He turns to see a pickup truck proudly flying the confederate flag. "The Devil Went Down to Georgia" blasts from the cab of the truck. Five young men hoot and holler as they close in on their prey. Each swings a bat or chain over his head. Before Paul can dive out of the way, a Louisville slugger smacks him in the back of the head, sending him face-first onto the pavement. He looks up to see the truck making a wide U-turn to head back toward him. He tries to get up but falls back, almost passing out.

"So, nigger, you want to stop racism, huh? Well, running ain't gonna do it," says the one holding the bloody bat in his dirty hands.

"Tell him, Jimbo ... Tell him what's gonna stop racism!" yells another over the radio.

"In time, Billy, in time. First we better show this buck what's gonna stop this so-called racism. Boys, shall we begin?" asks Jimbo as he slowly taps the bloody tip of the bat in his free hand. All at once they begin to beat the shit out of Paul. Each man concentrates on a specific body part. One guy gets particular joy out of repeatedly kicking him in the balls. Blood is everywhere. Paul's screams soon cease as the beating continues. After fifteen minutes of this they stop.

Breathing heavily, Jimbo says, "Now that we've showed this boy what's gonna stop racism let me tell you what is. One thing and one thing only is gonna stop it: violence. That's right, buck:

killing. 'Cuz we plan to wipe all you people real soon ...

"What 'bout the kikes and the spics, Jimbo?" one asks.

"Them too, baby, them too. Let's go, boys," says Jimbo.

All the guys spit and or piss on Paul's beaten body as they leave. They drive away to the sounds of the national anthem on their eight-track player.

Paul lies there motionless for thirty-six hours. On Sunday, exactly four weeks and six days into his run, he slowly starts to crawl toward the sounds of a huge mega mall. When he reaches the opening he stops, breathing heavily, exhausted from the effort. He is almost dead.

Soon a mother with her child approaches the body. "Don't touch him, baby ... he's dirty and nasty. All those people are," the mother says.

Her child breaks away from her mother and runs over to Paul. He opens his eyes and looks at the child before him.

He smiles. So does the child.

As the child bends over him, the mother screams bloody murder. With his last breath Paul whispers something to the child. She smiles and nods.

Paul dies.

The child begins to push her way through the crowd that has gathered. Her mother yells and screams for her to come back. The child turns to look at her mother for what she believes to be the last time. Their eyes lock for an instant, and then she turns to keep on running. She bumps into a small black boy. They stare at each other. In a movement that almost seems like slow motion, one child whispers something to the other. They both grin and turn to begin running ...

South.

... And a child shall lead them.

Chapter 12

TEMP, INC.

"I looove New York."

—Pinky

INTRODUCTION

Through the 1990s I worked for a local television station in New Jersey. I had taken the job because I had been through several business setbacks and just wanted a nine-to-five gig. I had spent the latter part of the 1980s working in film. The majority of it was in music videos, but I had worked as a second assistant director on Spike Lee's *School Daze* in 1986. I turned down working on *Tougher Than Leather*, Run DMC's feature debut, because I didn't like the script, but I kept busy just the same. I was asked in 1988 to help form a company centered on several black film directors. Well, as you can imagine things didn't work out as planned and I was left out on my ass. If they had, this would be a different book. Once again, my friend Clark Grain (he passed away in 1997 of sickle-cell anemia ... I still miss him) came to my aid. He told me about a gig at this television station. I interviewed and got the job. I would be working nights, but that was okay. I wanted privacy and a steady check, and this provided me with both.

I wound up working the overnight shift for seven years. Working 11 p.m. to 7 a.m. will definitely give a person a new outlook on life. People who have never worked it always tell you how cool it must be to have your days free to take care of business. The extra pay must be a nice perk. The drive must be a breeze because you're driving against traffic. They have a whole list of things, but what they're really thinking is: "This poor sap, working through the night—what kind of life is that for a human being?" This might be true, but there are many businesses that run 24-7-365. Television is a perfect example. Now, I'm not saying that it is quality TV, but it is television nonetheless. Someone has to be there to monitor the signal all the time.

I will tell you what I missed most when I was working nights. It's sleeping in your own bed at night. Some say that your body adjusts to the time change, but that's a lie. We as human beings were built to sleep at night. It's in our genes. What you do is adjust to the situation. Being single, I found it best to sleep in the morning, wake up about noon, do what had to be done, and take a nap before I went to work at 11 p.m. To this day I don't understand how married folk on that shift handled it. Gotta pay the bills. God bless them. I do remember one thing I did consistently: I would always count the hours of sleep I would get. It was a ritual. I would say to myself: "If I go to sleep right now I will get five hours of sleep." That sort of thing.

Anyway, I fell into a pattern and endured. I went to work and went home. I have to admit that I was a loner to a certain extent, but that was okay. I moved to the town that the station was in to make my commute shorter so I could sleep longer. I could walk or ride my bike to work in less than ten minutes. I wasn't writing much at all, but I was making money and paying my bills.

Several years passed as if they were days of the week. One day I got a call from my friend Butch Robinson, who told me that the short film *The Session* we had made had attracted someone who was interested in making it into a feature film. To make a long story short, the next several years were extremely busy. We had formed a production company called DROP Squad Pictures (DSP) with David Johnson and Eric Payne. The thing I will always remember is laughing our asses off constantly. As they say, "Those were the days, my friend. I thought they'd never end!" (Oops, the runner stumbled again.)

I would work at the TV station from 11 p.m. to 7 a.m., go into the office from 8 a.m. until 3 p.m., arrive home around 5 p.m., sleep until 10 p.m. and go back to the station. I had Monday and Tuesday off, so I was working seven days a week. I kept this up for three years. Well, it paid off when we finally got funding to turn our short film into a feature film in 1994. I quit my job and went off to Atlanta, GA, to make a feature film based on my idea. Let's just say things didn't go as planned (like I said earlier, this is another book entirely).

Anyway, to make a long story longer my days were very busy, with little time to hang out. What I started doing was having lunch at a restaurant called Gonzalez y Gonzalez (G&G) down in the village before I went home to get some sleep (special thanks to Maurice, Paulette and Lisa!). Over time I became friendly with several of the bartenders and waiters. One of them I really started to like. She was from England and we quickly became friends. If you're thinking that I wrote a story to get close to her, you're wrong. I wrote a short film to get close to her. She was an aspiring actress, like most waiters and waitresses in NYC, so this could be a break for her. I have always liked the fish-out-of-water device in films. She seemed to fall into this category, so the story almost wrote itself. The spark for this idea came to me while watching reruns of *The Mary Tyler Moore Show*—specifically the opening sequence. There was something about Mary throwing her hat up into the air at the end that I found interesting. I asked myself: "What if someone, an actress new to the Big Apple, had this enthusiasm and innocence at first but things didn't go as scripted?"

I had planned to shoot it on video that summer. It had a quirky feel to it that I liked a lot. I gave it to her when I finished. She liked it and said that she would play the lead. Right about then fate reared its ugly head. At DSP, we hit a very busy period producing infomercials and music videos. This hectic period lasted a couple of months, so I didn't have time to hang out at G&G. When I finally did return I learned that she had quit and moved on to another job.

Like before, I didn't get the girl, but I had another project finished. Who knew that not getting the woman would be so productive? I know it's a stretch, but like I said before: give a brother a break. Besides, rationalization is a wonderful thing.

TEMP, INC.

IN BLACK

The sound of a large bus changing gears explodes on the screen. After several moments, rising above the noise, the voice of a young woman enters our darkened frame. It is English, Cockney to be exact, and hip in its use of the language; however, a hint of innocence can be found if one listens hard enough.

> VOICE
> (dreamily)
> I can't believe it. New York! It's what I've dreamed of forever. They said I'd never do it. It took forever and every quid I could scrape together, but it's gonna pay off in spades, love. Just watch my smoke.

EXT. BUS/ROADWAY—DAY

The image of a spinning bus tire fills the frame. The CAM booms up the side of the bus and up to the window, revealing the young woman that the voice belongs to, ANDREA "PINKY" WARD, twenty-one, white, full of life. The young woman has a tint of pink in her hair and is dead to the world, sleeping off her long trip. Even while she sleeps a grin of accomplishment falls over her face.

PINKY
(still dreaming)
York ... just like I pictured it. If I can make it here. I can make it anywhere... IIIII LLOOOVE NNEEW-WYYOORRK ... New York, New York, it's a wonderful town, the Bronx is up and the Battery is down. New York, New York ...

INT. BUS—DAY
Pinky's singing is interrupted by the bus driver's voice.

BUS DRIVER (OC)
New York City, Port Authority. Next and final stop.

Pinky's eyes shoot open as the driver finishes his statement. She wipes the spit off her chin and the hair from her face. She strains in her seat, trying to see her future.

EXT. BUS—DAY
The bus pulls away from the camera. As it leaves the frame the camera turns and widens, revealing the NYC landscape.

EXT. PORT AUTHORITY/42ND ST—DAY
Pinky exits onto 42nd St. and 9th Ave. She is trying to balance her suitcase, a soft drink, several movie magazines and the latest issues of *People*, *Backstage*, the *National Enquirer* and *US*. She backs out into the busy sidewalk. She turns around to take in the hustle and bustle of an average New York day. She takes

several steps and drops her bags, throwing her arms up into the air.

PINKY
(yelling to NYC)
Watch out, New York ... here comes the latest and greatest thing to hit the great white way since the ... credit card and Ticketron. And I'm not gonna stop with old Broadway, no way. Movies, music videos, TV, music ... the sky's the limit. Forget garbage about keeping your feet on the ground, I'm reaching for the stars. I'm gonna make it after all ... (Mary Tyler Moore tune)

On this note, she throws her hat in the air. However, she fails to catch the hat, and it falls to the ground. As she reaches down to pick it up, a well-dressed older white man gives her ass a squeeze.

MAN
How much would be willing to charge for services?

Pinky jumps up, and without thinking slaps the man in the face, knocking him backward. She quickly grabs her stuff and runs off. She loses herself in the crowd as the man rants and raves.

EXT. BUILDING—DAY
Pinky walks up to the building, looking at a letter that she holds

in her hands. It reads:

Miss Andrea Ward
118 Hanover St
London, England

Dear Miss, Mrs., Ms_____,

Congratulations! You have been chosen to be the first participant in the first annual bimonthly Professional Acting Scholarship. This award means that you are steps away from living the Lifestyles of the Rich and Famous. Our school has been a home to the likes of M. Streep, L. Strasberg and C. Grant. As an awardee you are entitled to six months of intensive training by our professionals, to be followed by several starring roles in abstract adaptations of Shakespeare's works. Please come by our offices in New York to claim your award. All expenses will be repaid after you pass our physical requirements.

See you in Hollywood,
Jock Dubious
President
Dubious Entertainment

Pinky smiles when she rereads the letter for what must be the hundredth time. She looks up when she hears her name being called and sees a man leaning out of a window.

JOCK
(French accent/waving madly)
Mon ami, I am so glad you came. I recognize you
from your head shots. Your timing is impeccable.
Please come up to my office.

As she walks toward the door it buzzes. When she grabs the
handle the door stops buzzing. She presses the doorbell and
waits. The door buzzes again, but catches her off guard. She
tries to beat the buzzer in vain. With one hand on the door
handle and the other on the buzzer, she rings it again. The pull
flies open, causing her to fall on her ass. She quickly gets up and
runs through the doorway.

INT HALLWAY OF DUBIOUS APT—DAY
POV MS of Pinky's hand knocking on Dubious Entertainment
Door. The door swings open, revealing a short hallway. One
side is covered with books; the other is covered with posters
from various movies. A poster of *Kiss of the Spider Woman* has
Jock's name written in felt pen over the real producer's name.
The CAM moves through the hallway toward a larger room in
the back. As she moves down the hallway she can see Jock on
the phone.

JOCK
(Brooklyn accent)
You get that ho to do whatever it takes to get the
fuckin' shot. I got it: tell her that her husband will get

the stills from her phys—

He looks up to see Pinky standing in the entranceway of his office.

JOCK (cont.)
Listen ... Just tell her that it would do her career a world of good. Besides, snakes are God's creatures too.

Pinky looks at Jock, confused.

PINKY
Wha ... What happened to your accent?

Jock puts down the phone and walks over to her and circles her as he speaks.

JOCK
(thinking)
My huh? ... Accent? ... Oh that—I was practicing for an upcoming role. You've heard of the play *Camelot*?

She nods.

JOCK (cont.)
That's good—student of the arts to boot. So sit down and tell me about yourself. I'm kinda in the middle of

screening my latest adaptation of Shakespeare's *King Lear*.

Pinky's face lights up hearing this. He leads her over to the sofa, where they sit down. The TV is facing Jock. He stares past her as she talks.

PINKY
(gaining confidence)
Well, I've done many of the classics in regional theater in England. In my prep school I was voted most likely to succeed ...

Jock sits there nodding his head, captivated by what is on the screen in front of him.

PINKY (cont.)
My favorite play is *My Fair Lady*. I played Eliza Doolittle ...

Jock's eyes light up hearing this.

JOCK
(cutting her off)
My Fair Lady, right, right. I got it! We do it with lesbos. Oh yeah, I love it. The babe teaches her to be a better lover! Now *that's* got legs.

Before she can react to this statement, he continues.

JOCK (cont.)
This is my favorite part in *King Lear*. This is when he
takes it in the ass.

She turns to look at the screen and sees a X-rated film. She covers her eyes.

JOCK
(still looking at the screen)
This film will go down in the annals of the porn film
industry. So tell me—I know that it is early in your
film career and you ain't had any of my school's training—but how 'bout taking a stab at the role? Ya
know—the lesbo Doolittle thing?

Pinky slowly takes her hand away from her face and looks at
Jock, then the screen and then Jock again.

PINKY
(unbelieving)
You want me to do that ... that's not acting, that's ...
that's ...

Jock throws his hands in the air.

JOCK

That's showbiz, baby. Now about that physical the
letter talks about?

Jock reaches for Pinky's shirt and is greeted with a right cross.
He goes down like a sack of potatoes. Pinky runs out of the
apartment.

JOCK
(in pain)
I—I—I hope ya know dat you won't   be   reimbursed
for your expenses ... *Ugghhh.*

INT. HALLWAY/ANOTHER BUILDING—DAY

Pinky walks down the hallway looking at *Backstage*, an industry
newspaper, trying to find the office of a particular agency. She
spies the door she wants and approaches it. Before knocking,
she fixes herself up. She knocks on the door and waits. Nothing.
Pinky takes out a copy of her resume and pictures. She slips it
underneath the door and walks away. She turns back to see her
material slide back from under the door into the hallway. She
walks back to it and pushes it inside. She turns away. Pinky
smiles when it doesn't return and walks away. At the elevator
she sees it sitting outside the office again and runs back. She
jams it back inside, only to see it being pushed out. A push of
war develops. It goes back in. Thinking that she has won, she
hears something being ripped. It returns in two pieces.

INT. YET ANOTHER HALLWAY—DAY

Pinky enters another hallway, looking more determined than ever. She knocks on a door labeled "Actor's Associates." She waits awhile for the door to open. It doesn't. She takes a deep breath and sighs. She takes out her picture and slides it under the door and prepares for it to come out. It doesn't. As she begins to walk away she hears voices from behind the door.

                    VOICE #1
                (whispering, male)
Whatever you do, don't answer the door. Remember what happened last time, dick brain?

                    VOICE #2
                (high-pitched whine)
How should I know that we were supposed to pay taxes every year? You told me that we were incorporated or something. What do you think—I'm a M.F.A. or something?

                    VOICE #1
M.F.A.! M.F.A.! It's not M.F.A., you jackass. It's M.B.A. And you couldn't spell it, let alone earn one.

                    VOICE #2
You're always yelling at me. Why can't you just be nice like Mom said to be?

                    VOICE #1
Mom! She was a dickhead too!

Pinky backs away from the door, dropping her resume and pictures on the floor, and slowly walks away.

EXT RUNDOWN HOTEL—AFTERNOON
Pinky walks up the street toward her hotel. She is upset and confused by what has happened to her over the last couple of days.

PINKY
This can't be happening. Whatever happened to wanting something bad enough and having it happen? Whatever happened to ... to ...

Out of the background a hand shoots in and spins her around. The hotel desk manager confronts her.

MANAGER
... paying your rent ... being responsible ... following through. I can spot a dead beat—hell, I can smell 'em a mile off. And sister, you reek to high heaven.

On this note he drops her bags on the ground and turns and walks away. Pinky picks up her bags and walks away feeling like Felix Unger from *The Odd Couple*.

EXT EAST VILLAGE CORNER—AFTERNOON
Pinky stops on the corner and rests. A person eating a hot dog walks by her. She looks at the hot dog with hunger in her eyes. She reaches into her pockets and pulls out nothing but lint. She

walks over to the hot dog vendor.

PINKY
(timidly)

Hey, mate, let me have one with some of that, and that there ... He preps the dog as she instructs. It is filled to the brim with chili, onions, sauerkraut, mustard and ketchup, and overflows, dripping on the ground. As she reaches for it the vendor pulls it away.

VENDOR

No money, no doggy. No kidding ...

Pinky smiles, thinking that this might help. He looks at the dog, then Pinky. He takes a bite out of it and throws the rest in the garbage. She walks away.

EXT. STREET CORNER—AFTERNOON

Wandering through the streets, lost and dejected, she absent-mindedly takes a leaflet from a man wearing dark glasses, a floppy hat and an overcoat. She glances at the paper and drops it, then spots the very first line: NEED MONEY? EARN IT FAST!!!! She quickly picks it up and unfolds it.

PINKY
(reading)

Need money? Earn it fast, fast, fast. Answer these

simple questions and you will be well on your way to your destiny. Can you type? No. Can you write and/or transcribe shorthand? No. Can you word process? No. Can you file? No. Whether you answered yes or no to any of these questions, you're Temp, Incorporated material. There's no way you can lose ... so call now!

Pinky looks over her shoulder to see that the man who handed her the leaflet is nowhere to be seen. She sees a payphone and runs to it. She searches for change, but has none. At the bottom of the paper it reads: DON'T WORRY, YOU CAN CALL COLLECT, SO CALL NOW. 1-800-555-6666. She quickly dials the number. While she waits to be connected, she straightens her hair and clothing.

VOICE
(female)
Temporary, Incorporated. How can I help you?
PINKY
Hi, umm, I saw your leaflet about work and I'm ... well, interested.

Silence.

VOICE
Welcome to the Temp, Incorporated family. You have taken the first step to making your life fun and

rewarding ...

                    PINKY

But I answered no to all the questions.

                    VOICE

You mean you can't type?

                    PINKY

              (slightly embarrassed)

No ... but I ...

                    VOICE

Can you word process?

                    PINKY

No.

                    VOICE

Well, how about shorthand?

                    PINKY

Well, it depends on the ... no.

                    VOICE

File?

                    PINKY

              (apologetically)

Nuh-uh.

                    VOICE

You can write, can't you?

                    PINKY

Of course I can! What do think I am?

                    VOICE

                 (sighing)

I'm glad you got one right. Now, as I was saying ...

Welcome to the Temp, Incorporated family. You have just taken the first step to a fun and rewarding life. Let's see here ... Oh, you're in luck, we have a job for tonight on the Upper East Side. 888 E. 91st Street. Report to a Mr. Johnson.

She quickly scribbles down the address.

> PINKY
> (skeptical)
> I ... I ... I don't know about this.
> VOICE
> It pays cash ... two hundred fifty for five hours of work. Taking notes, helping out with some very light filing. If you don't ...
> PINKY
> I'll take it, it's mine!
> VOICE
> Good, and remember that you are a representative of the Temp, Incorporated family, so make us proud. Good luck.

Pinky hangs up with a new lease on life. She grabs her bags and starts out on her journey. She glances up at the street sign, which says E. 12th St. She takes a deep breath and starts walking.

EXT. BROWNSTONE—NIGHT

Pinky has long lost the slide in her glide and the cut in her strut. One could say that she is almost limping. However, seeing her destination renews her energy. She walks up the steps, straightens up and rings the bell.

INT. LIBRARY—NIGHT

She is led into the room by the maid, who instructs her to have a seat. Pinky sits and waits .... and waits and waits. She glances away from the door for a moment. When she turns back, Mr. Johnson, fiftyish, very distinguished, is standing in the doorway. He walks toward her and stops in front of her.

MR. JOHNSON

How do you do? My name is Johnson—Rogfurt Johnson of the Greenwich Court Johnsons. Let's get started, shall we? It's getting late. There is an envelope on that table. It holds the money you are owed. I like to get the finances out of the way. Now, the job at hand. I'd like to dictate a letter. She pulls out a pencil and pad of paper from her bag.

MR. JOHNSON (cont.)

No, no, no. Please use these. They find that these work out the best in the end.

He produces an expensive mechanical pencil and pad out of thin air. She takes them and drops them. She picks them up and looks around for Mr. Johnson. She looks around the room and doesn't see him.

PINKY
(questioning)
Mr ...?

His hand touches her shoulder. She jumps out of her chair, turning to him.

MR. JOHNSON
Shall we begin?

Pinky slowly sits down, keeping an eye on Mr. Johnson as he walks to the bar. With his back to her, he slowly pours himself a brandy and then quickly turns around.

MR. JOHNSON
(thinking and drinking)
Dear Mr. Babbit. Concerning our meeting of the fourteenth of this month, I do agree with points A, B, C and D. However, point E is a problem. I feel so strongly about this that I'd like to kill you.

She doesn't hear any of this because she is too busy writing. However, when she comes to the word "kill" she stops. She looks up to see him puffing calmly on a pipe.

MR. JOHNSON
(calmly)
Let's see, where was I, miss ... ah?
PINKY
Andrea Ward.
MR. JOHNSON
Well?
PINKY
(unsure)
Miss Andrea Ward of the Manchester Wards?
MR. JOHNSON
(impatient)
The letter, Miss Ward, the letter. Where were we?
PINKY
(surprised)
Oh, uh ... You were about to kill him ... sir.
MR. JOHNSON
Oh yes, okay ... I'd like to tear your ears off so you
can't hear yourself scream.

He walks over to her and looks over her shoulder as she writes.

MR. JOHNSON
Presently I'm dictating this memo to my next victim.

He quickly closes his hands around her neck and squeezes the
life from her body. She looks up at him to see that he is dressed
in the same dark glasses and hat as the man on the street who

had given her the leaflet.

INT. TEMP, INC. OFFICE—NIGHT
A hand reaches for the ringing phone.

VOICE
(female)
Hello, Temp, Incorporated. May I help you? Oh,
Mr. Johnson, and how are we this evening? Good,
good, and how did the girl work out this time?
Wonderful! What else can we help you with? A
Spanish girl … And you want us to pick her out this
time? No problem. And how do you plan to kill her
this time? Decapitation? I love it! We'll send someone over this weekend. And remember: for all your
serial-killer needs, keep us in mind.

She whistles a happy tune and places the phone in the cradle.

Chapter 13
A Random Dream Thought ...

SAVANT

... From day one he knew he was different.

He began speaking at eight months and never stopped. He had a lot on his mind and he had a duty to tell people about it.

At first it was like a party trick. His folks would drag him out at family gatherings to play the piano or recite classic poems from memory. He didn't mind ...

But then one day things changed ... His parents bought a computer. He discovered the Internet, giving him access to all the information in the world at his fingertips. It didn't take him long to hack into places and hard drives that he wasn't supposed to be in ... but they held information that he needed to grow ... to change into what he was to become.

He was different, and he knew it. He found through the Internet others who were like him, and they formed a news group using such advanced encryption that anyone who stumbled onto it would see it as gibberish. Together they had plans that would change the world in a direction that no one would imagine. Everyone would be equalized in all areas of life. No one would suffer the indignities of poverty, racism or bias anymore ... Harmony would be achieved. It was so easy. All the answers were right there to see. All you had to do was open your eyes.

They divided their group into several areas of expertise: artistic, scientific, financial, and sociological. Together they came up with a timeline that would propel humanity a thousand years into the future within a ten-year period. Evolution within a half a generation.

Then things started to change. It was slow to see at first, but it was a force to be dealt with. One by one the group of twelve dropped out of sight. Over a span of ten years only he was left. At first he tried to keep things together, but soon real life started to creep into his situation. He graduated from high school, not at the top, but in the lower third of his class. You see, he was diagnosed with being hyperactive so Ritalin and lithium were given to him, slowing the brain process. He couldn't concentrate, so he just slowed down. He knew what was happening but couldn't stop it. The medication took away the pain of not achieving what he knew was his destiny.

He fell into the cycle of society. Graduating high school, passing up college for a job on a high-tech assembly line for computer parts.

Oh, there were times when he would have strokes of genius, but the medication took care of those. He would write them down as they came, to only look them over as if some other person had written them. It would be years before he would understand them and then apply them, not only to him but also to society. Because of his lack of understanding he took a lot of time off of work. They didn't understand him so they let him go. But it didn't matter.

One day he decided to stop taking his medication. At first it was a rollercoaster ride, sending him into a whirlwind of emotions. But he kept to his regime of exercise and meditation and things soon cleared up. For the first time in years his mind was free and clear.

He tried to contact the former members of the news group but they all denied knowing him.

It wasn't long before his monthly bills caught up with him and he had to take a job as a computer repairman at Best Buy. He decided to write down his ideas and the ideas of his group for future generations. He met a woman who understood his moods and got her pregnant. She had a baby girl. He knew his chance was over, but something was different because he was happy for the first time in his life ...

His little girl began speaking at five months ...

Chapter 14

YOUTH IS WASTED

ON THE YOUNG

"Susie's disappearance causes Jorge to almost go insane."

—Narrator

INTRODUCTION

These next two stories, "Youth Is Wasted on the Young" and "The End of the Beginning," were written while I was working on the overnight shift of the television station. I was on one of my writing jags and couldn't wait to get to the typewriter. There are two things that stick in my mind about writing these two pieces on the job. The first is that my particular job at the station was being a Master Control operator. I'm the guy who lets technical difficulties slide while running around like crazy trying to find the problem. I compare it to being on a darkened rollercoaster ride. There are times when the ride is smooth, but you know in the back of your mind that a dip is coming. The other thing about the job is that you had to pay attention at all times. This, of course was made more difficult by the fact that it was 4:30 in the morning and you were in the third hour of the Home Shopping Network or the zillionth airing of that Juiceman infomercial.

Anyway, the only decent typewriter was in an audio room down the hall. Once again the problem was in the timing. The Home Shopping Network aired from 2 a.m. to 6 a.m. during the week. Now this wasn't the problem (and as Dennis Miller says, "I don't want to go off on a rant, but ..."), but whatever happened to the late-late movie on television stations these days? Ever since the invention of home shopping and the infomercial, late-night television sucks. Thank God for cable. Okay, I'm back. Anyway, we had to roll three breaks per hour for home shopping so I would leave the door open to the Master Control room, turn up the volume and write like crazy. When I would hear the theme music I would run out of the room and down the hall and roll the break. I never missed. Well, almost never ...

Now that I have shown you my writing process, let's talk about the spark. What it all comes down to is *Silence of the Lambs*. I had gone on a date and seen the movie (and no, it's not the best first-date movie. It's like taking her to see *Fatal Attraction* or *Kramer vs. Kramer*). It blew me away. For about a week I couldn't get it out of my mind. I went back and rented the film *Manhunter*, based on Thomas Harris's book *Red Dragon*. I even read both of the books. Well, this got me thinking about a crime thriller with a twist. Late one night at the station it hit me, so I wrote it.

YOUTH IS WASTED
ON THE YOUNG

Our story opens like stories did for a lot of new Americans at the Immigration and Naturalization Service. Jorge, thirty-five years old, Colombian, dark-skinned, works his way through the long lines and paperwork associated with coming to live in this country. All the things that are happening to him are new and strange, yet wonderful. He is about to begin the first day of the rest of his life.

To meet him at the office is his family, which has been over here for some time now. He had worked hard to make this a reality. Working at jobs he hated to save up money that would give his family a fighting chance in this world. Many of his friends had done the opposite. They would come over to America and work to bring their families over. This, however, brought with it many problems. The biggest is temptation. Many would get over here and be seduced by the wonders of this open society. He would do it differently. He would do it right. Several cousins, along with his adored younger sister, Ina, twenty-one years old, gorgeous, engulf him as he gets his final stamp of approval from Uncle Sam. One of the last things the officials tell the graduation class of 1995 is that they may have hard time adjusting to our culture. After getting his green card he holds it up like it is his ticket to the future.

As they take the subway to their Queens apartment building, Jorge looks around at the people on the train and sees things that he would never have dreamt of. A homeless person sings and dances for the patrons, ignored by the wealthy-looking people who have their noses buried in their newspapers. A man and woman passionately kiss and fondle each other as if they are in the privacy of their own bedroom. He looks over at his family, to see that they are obviously used to these sights and sounds. He thinks that this place is nuts. He remembers that there were times when he doubted his decision to come over here but it was his mother's dying wish to bring the family over to America to start a new life. Plus, he missed Ina. She was the light of his life.

Once in the apartment, Ina tells him that she is working as a maid in a house in Greenwich, Connecticut. Her boss has really taken a liking to her and has gotten her a partial scholarship to continue her education. This makes the family very happy because she would be the first one to go to a community college, or any college for that matter. Jorge beams upon hearing this.

During the day, when everyone is at work, Jorge walks around the city. He tries to take in all there is to see but finds it difficult. That day he gets taken in by a three-card monty game and loses most of his money. When he tries to get it back he is beaten up. The cops come in and arrest both of them. Down at the station, the police discover that they cannot talk to him because of the language difference. They call in Nancy Richardson, thirty, Colombian, to translate. It turns out that they are from the same region in Columbia and talk very easily about what happened to him. During their conversion an officer comes running into the office and whispers something in Nancy's ear. They both run out into the squad room, where a group of cops discuss something important. Jorge watches through the wire-reinforced glass. They seem upset about what has happened. She returns and tells him that another victim of the ritual cannibal murders has been found. There have been ten so far, and they don't have a clue as to where to start looking. All the victims have been no older than eighteen, full of life, with everything to live for.

Over the next several weeks, Jorge and Nancy start hanging out together. She shows him the sights of NYC, explaining them to him in his own language. The killings also continue to happen ... about one per week.

One day Jorge gets a chance to meet Ina's boss, Mr. Alex Haven, fiftyish, white, at his home in Greenwich. He had invited all the families of his housing staff for a cookout. Jorge takes Nancy to the affair. Upon meeting Mr. Haven, Jorge senses something strange about the man. He never shakes hands, but appears to be very friendly with everyone. During the course of the day he gets a chance to go off by himself and discovers several artifacts from his homeland, many of which have ancient religious meanings. Surprising him, Nancy and Haven come walking in and begin to explain the artifacts while Nancy translates for Jorge. For many years he has had a fascination with the older cultures of the world and feels that we could learn a lot from them.

That next week, Ina disappears, which causes Jorge to almost go insane. The police find out that Haven dropped her off at the Metro North train station that evening and returned home. Something about the story doesn't ring true to Jorge. He finally convinces Nancy that Haven may have had something to do with the killings and his sister's disappearance. He tells her that when he was a child his grandfather told him of the old ways, many of which involved cannibalism. These rituals were used by the high priests to attain eternal life so that they might better serve their gods forever. Cannibalism was an important part of that ritual because the eating of live flesh would allow the eater to absorb the life force from the victim, allowing them to retain their youth and strength. Jorge investigates the ritual angle by going to several old men in the Colombian community. He discovers that they believed that the killings are an exact duplication of what transpired centuries ago. They must be stopped. Nancy discovers that each of the victims had some type of connection to a group of businessmen, all of whom went to the same grad school and received their MBAs in the same year.

One night they go up the Havens' abode and see a lot of cars in the lot next to the main house. They sneak in and listen to the meeting that is going on in the basement of the house. The men and women talk of eternal life and how money has become the new god in today's world. Nancy recognizes a member of the group—he is the young detective who is investigating the murders. They begin to chant a prayer that Jorge recognizes as preparation for dinnertime. They watch as Ina is brought out and strapped down to the dining-room table. Just as they are about to eat, Jorge and Nancy burst in and disrupt the feast. However, they are both captured and tied up by the young executives. Nancy replaces Ina on the dining table. She will be served as a second course. Jorge strains against his bonds as his love is about to be served as human sushi. He yells out something in his native tongue, freezing them in their place. Soon his voice is joined by the voices of others. These do not come from the yuppies, but from his countrymen who have come to help their brother. An all-out brawl ensues in which his countrymen use their native kickboxing technique developed by slaves long ago. Jorge and Haven wind up fighting on the roof, using several weapons from his country. Jorge is wounded, but winds up killing Haven.

Chapter 15

THE END OF THE BEGINNING

"I think, therefore I am."
—Cell

INTRODUCTION

Before I introduce this story, I want to say something about writing all these Dream Thoughts. For me it all comes down to one thing. Yes, the magic and or spark that comes from the first pass is truly exciting, but it's the rewriting that gives them their sparkle. This might seem obvious, but whoever said "The art in writing is rewriting" was absolutely correct. Everyone has their own technique but what works for me is doing the first pass on a computer. Through the years I have found that I am writing so fast that I leave out words or whole thoughts. I attribute this to wanting to get the idea down before I forget it. I go back and print it out, make notations and return to the computer. This can go on for weeks or months, until I reach the point where I am satisfied with the final product. Since I'm the worst person in the world with grammar I have several people whom I let read what I write (thank you, Electa Brown, Janet McGill and my mom and dad from the bottom of my heart). Once this is completed, if it's a script, I hold an informal reading. This consists of getting some of my acting friends together and listening to my words. I'll tell you that hearing your words, especially the dialogue, for the first time is an eye-opening experience. If the people are good, they will add inflections, pauses and a sense of style to what you have written that may not have been there when you wrote. I can remember holding a reading for *The Trilogy* when one of the actors read a line. It was one word: "Unholy." I know it sounds simple, but his timing and tone blew me away.

To finish the process, I record the reading and listen to it. What I look for is the reaction of the other actors. If they react in the right way, I know that it's right. If not, I have to make a change. I got this idea after reading a bio of Frank Capra. He would record each screening of his films and use the audience's reaction as a cue to change something.

This story started with the title and some help from Steven King. He had just released the unabridged version of *The Stand*. I had read the earlier version, but this one was phenomenal. The scope was bigger and the ending was inventive and unexpected. Once again it got me thinking. One thing that I was really interested in was writing my version of the end of the world. I thought and thought and came up with squat. I was at home at night looking at American Movie Classics when the movie *The Beginning of the End* came on. It's a 1950s B-movie classic about these giant grasshoppers that try to take over the world. The movie itself is one of the many films they made back then that focused on the dangers of the atomic bomb. (One of the best was *Them!*, about giant ants that try to take over the world.)

Well, the combination of reading the book and watching the movie got me started. Late one night at the station it all came together. I put on my rollerblades and got to work. Three nights later, I came up with this.

THE END OF THE BEGINNING

It all started with what was called the strangest thing ever to hit humanity ... but it was only the end of the beginning. It wasn't that it hadn't happened before; this was something else all together.

The *NY Post* reported it with the following headline: SNOW BIZ TAKES LA BY STORM?

Now, snow was something that has happened in Southern California every century or so, but this was just plain weird. In a period of twelve hours, three feet of snow dropped on the left coast. Of course, the new age folk thought this was a sign from one of their hundred spiritual guides. And of course people still thought that they were just plain nuts.

Over a span of thirty days the weather all around the world started to act up. The Antarctic reached temperatures of ninety degrees, but before the polar ice caps could melt it dropped eighty degrees in less than six hours. That was when things really started to get strange.

Julio wakes from his slumber like someone has punched him in the stomach. Before the scream leaves his lips he slams his hand over his mouth so as not to wake Sonya, his wife of ten years. After the pain subsides, he softly slides out of bed, almost stepping on his pit bull, Mr. Peepers. Being a pit bull, the beast almost takes off his leg in one chomp. He never did like the dog, but Sonya adores the animal so he tries to put up with it, teeth and all.

After recovering from his near-fatal error, he quietly showers and dresses for the day. As he prepares, he flicks on the television to hear of the strange occurrences that seem to inhabit the news. While shaving, he almost slits his throat as his eye catches video news footage of the latest thing to happen to the world at large. It seems as though scientists have found that, on a microscopic level, an entire species of paramecium has just vanished from existence. There is no explanation for this phenomenon. Before the story is over, Julio is out the door and on his way to work.

A little background on our Julio is called for. He was born in Spanish Harlem in May, 1955. As he grew up he took a path that many people take who grow up in that kind of situation: drugs, gangs and violence.

When he was twenty-five years old, after a hard night of warring with a rival gang, he was arrested for driving a stolen vehicle. He tried to explain to the police that he was too tired to walk home after a long night. The judge gave him one year in Rahway State Prison, as well as six months of community service. After serving his time he was told that the only job he could get was a book returner in the New York Public Library. He had no choice in the matter. At first he hated working in the joint. Every once in a while he would look at the books he was putting away. Sidney Sheldon, Robert Ludlum, Karl Marx and the Bob Vila book series. All these books bored him to no end. Then one day he happened to glance at a book entitled

Computers and You: A Guide to APL. Something about it got him really excited. He read the book in one sitting. The truly amazing thing to him was that he understood every word of it. In fact, he saw ways that would improve the language. It was as though a light had clicked on in his darkened brain. Over a period of three years he got his GED, BS and PhD in computer science. The problem that lay before him was twofold: his Hispanic ancestry and the fact that he had gotten his degrees via the mail. The only job he could get that interested him was a janitorial gig in a think tank located in the United Nations building.

On the subway on his way to his job at Dream Think, Inc. (DTI), Julio's mind races with the possible answers to the happenings of the last month. These new developments have wiped out all his other theories of a hole in the ozone layer or the cooling of the earth's core. This new element threw him for a loop. As he walks down the street he hardly takes notice of the abundance of soothsayers that seem to be popping up around the city. He almost knocks down a guy who carries a sign and spouts rhetoric about how Pee-wee Herman is the antichrist. Julio puts this out of his mind and enters the plain, unremarkable entrance to DTI located beneath the UN. In the elevator he runs into Gloria "My favorite organ is anything on the male body" Levy, who is assistant to the chairman of the organization. She has told him on many occasions how she is dying to try a Latin man. Julio tries to stay away from her, except when he needs information, like today. As she tries to run her fingers through his jet-black hair she tells him how all the brainaics are stumped. She goes on to say that the thing that they are really scared of is that it seems the food chain, starting at the bottom, is disappearing. Julio jumps as her hand firmly squeezes his ass. Another assistant walks toward them, which gives him a chance to get away.

He opens his office door and enters, closing it behind him. The interior looks like any other janitor's office, save for one thing: behind one of the bookcases is a false wall. He goes to it and enters his real office. Inside are no less than twenty computers, all running programs. He shuts all of them off and lies down on the hammock in the middle of the room. His mainframe is voice-activated, and he asks it to run a program using a database to correlate all of the events of the last several days. As the computer works on that problem, his beeper goes off. It's the chairman.

Outside of the office he hears people screaming at each other in several languages. He knocks softly and enters at Gloria's request. She asks him to clean up the broken glass that was thrown by Dr. Spangler. Without being noticed he goes about his business listening to what these learned men have to say. What he hears both frightens him and excites him. They talk and yell about the recent events. Dr. Chajide says that that the events must be biochemical in nature, due to some type of disturbance on a molecular level. Old Doc Smithy calls this idea "horse hockey," because the weather changes happened way before the disappearance of the one-celled organisms.

Suddenly the room is alive with the sounds of screaming voices. Through all this Julio looks over at Dr. Bantu of the Institute of Timbuktu, who sits quietly amid the chaos. He seems to be praying or something. The chairman quiets the greatest minds the world has ever seen to ask if anyone has anything new to add. Dr. Bantu, in a soft and gentle voice, tells the room that he believes that there is no scientific reason for what is happening. It just is. Everyone in the room screams bloody murder at this statement and continues to fight. Through it all, Julio locks eyes with the good doctor and sees him mouth a single word: "Shalamar." He smiles, and then is hit in the face with a right cross thrown by old Doc Smitty. Julio leaves the room with one word on his mind.

He runs down to his office. The mainframe has just finished the program he had asked for. He tells it to file that information in a temporary folder and to find the root definition of the word *Shalamar*. The computer goes silent for a minute, thinking. Julio bites his lower lip as he waits. The computer tells him that the meaning of the word in the doctor's language is "rebirth." This stumps him. He lies down on his hammock and has a bottle of suds. The mainframe recites the information IM its temp folder concerning the events that have transpired over the past thirty-one days, seventeen hours, thirty-four minutes and thirteen seconds. As he listens, something from his childhood comes to mind. All at once he sits up and tells the computer to stop.

It does.

He asks one simple question: Has this ever happened before? The computer searches for the answer.

No.

Damn, he thinks to himself. He then asks it to search all the data banks, both friendly and unfriendly.

It does.

Yes, the computer replies.

The answer excites him. Explain. It tells him that this has happened has happened two other times in the recorded history of the planet. These two occurrences fit into the parameters of its previous search:

I. 40,000 BC. There was a great disaster that wiped out all the inhabitants of the world. The first Ice Age engulfed the planet, destroying everything in its wake.

II. 10,000 BC. This disaster destroyed the planet by flood. It was written that one family survived in a homemade ark, which carried every species of animal two by two. Noah's Ark.

As a child he had always wondered how could all the animals fit on one ship, but now he understands. What if most of the animals had begun to disappear, decimating their numbers? Now *that* would be doable. Julio looks at the glowing screen in front of him in awe. He alone has figured out what is happening. The end of the world. He sits there for what seems like a lifetime. Then the computer asks him if there would be anything else. He asks it to hypothesize why this is happening now. Using this new info as the basis for its equation, the computer comes up with the theory that, due to our nature and the depletion of resources, the earth is regenerating itself. Basically it was set up to be self-cleaning. The process seems to happen every 20 million years, or when it feels the need. Julio is surprised to find that he is not panicking. In fact, a feeling of peace settles over him.

Knowing that there is nothing that he could do to save the earth as we know it, he decides to do something to help the next inhabitants of the planet. He decides to document the final moments of our world and to place them in a time capsule.

First he decides to bring his wife into his computer bunker. As he dials her number he turns on the television and sees that every nation is blaming the other for what is happening. Small wars have started to break out all over. When his wife answers, he tells her what has happened and what he plans to do. She tells him that she has known about this for some time now because, unlike him, she goes to church. She says that her pastor told his flock that science is to blame for what has happened. This is God's way of paying those smartasses back for what they have done to God's people. She tells him that the only place she is going is to her church to pray for her soul. As for him, since he is part of the problem, he should die like the rest of the sinners. She hangs up. Julio cries, knowing in his heart that she may be right. But this will not stop him from his destiny.

He goes out to buy as much food and drink as possible to sustain himself through the ordeal that is to come. On the outside of the UN, people have begun writing slogans on the walls: "GOD'S WILL BE DONE." "THIS IS THE END OF THE BEGINNING OF HUMANKIND." "SCIENCE SUCKS!"

He returns quickly with his supplies and locks himself in. He sets up his computers to scan the wire services for news on what is happening in the world.

PRESIDENT DECLARES ALL OF UNITED STATES A DISASTER AREA.

TROOPS ENTER EVERY MAJOR CITY TO KEEP LAW AND ORDER.

SUICIDE RATE LEAPS BY 1000 PERCENT.

WHERE HAVE ALL THE ANIMALS GONE?

WORLD CHURCH LEADERS AGREE ON ONE THING: IT'S ALL OVER!

BUILDINGS IN EVERY MAJOR CITY BEGIN TO CRUMBLE.

THE FAT LADY SINGS ...

Five million years after the earth has cooled itself down, a small puddle of water forms in a large crater. After a while it seems to grow in size. If one had the ability to somehow get inside the cell structure of one particular cell they would hear a faint, almost dreamlike voice repeating the same thing over and over:

I THINK, THEREFORE I AM ... I THINK, THEREFORE I AM ...

And the circle of life begins again.

Chapter 16

GARVEY HIGH '95

INTRODUCTION

I wrote this story as a short film in 1992. I wanted some material that Butch Robinson and I could shoot in New Jersey for no money. I was looking at my high school yearbook one day and got an idea. I was going to base the film on two women who randomly meet each other and discover that they graduated from the same high school in the same year. I needed it to have a twist or two, so I came up with several that seemed to work.

Butch and I worked on the draft and finished it. We called a couple of friends of ours and cast them in the project (I do want to thank them for working with us). We only shot about five pages of it and stopped. I can't tell you why, but that's what happened.

This past year (2015), I rewrote it as a stage play and it was performed in the Sankofa and Fringe festivals in Rochester, NY. I would like to thank David Shakes, Dede Gause, Sheila Rankin and Chris Fields for working with me to get it done.

GARVEY HIGH '95

INT. PAULA'S APT—DAY

In black, we hear the voice of PAULA SUGARMAN. She is engrossed in a heavy telephone conversation with one of her many suitors.

PAULA (VO)

Yes, Dusty, I got the flowers and the candy too. Oh, and that so-called diamond bracelet you gave me was just wonderful. No, no, I wasn't surprised to get the plane tickets either. Remember, I did have to ask for them, right? And I really thought you loved me ... Did you hear that? Was that mine or yours? Be a dear and hang on will you? Great.

The lights come up onstage as Paula presses the phone button down to switch to the other call.

PAULA (contd.)

Yes, Peter ... uh-huh ... Well, you tell that son of a bitch that his shit company and his profits are mine, and his ass is mine too. I'd rather dazzle them with brilliance than dazzle them with bullshit. Tell him that or I'll get someone who can.

She slams the receiver down and the phone rings again. She grabs it.

> PAULA (contd.)
>
> Baby, you still there? I'm sorry about that. There it goes again. I know, I'm such a social butterfly, right? Yes, uh-huh, my favorite position is sixty-nine. You know that. I'll talk to you later. Bye. [Clicks line] Anton, is that you? How you doin'? ... That's good. And how's big Al doin'? You're not keeping him up nights, are you? Oh, I love you too, baby ... And I love the new car you gave me too. But the GPS and DVD player don't work right. I want another one. No, not the GPS or the DVD, I want the new red one this time. Next year's model. Work on that, will ya?

There is a loud knock on her front door. She looks over at it.

> PAULA (contd.)
>
> I know you love me, but I can't drive love. Wait a minute, baby, there's someone knocking on my door.

She sets the phone down and walks over to the door. She opens it to see YASEEN NOURI standing there.

PAULA (contd.)

Can I help you?

YASEEN

Hi, I'm Yaseen Nouri and I'm with Black Starline Film Works. We're trying to raise funds from concerned art patrons for our upcoming projects. What we have planned for the first half of the year is ...

PAULA

(interrupting)

Yes, right, I'm sure that you have big plans but I get seasick on cruises and I don't stand in line at the movies. So I don't think I can help you.

YASEEN

(friendly)

No, no, no, I think you misunderstand what I'm saying. Black Starline is a consortium of black artists, film makers and technicians who have abandoned the traditional methods of production and distribution. We think that the only way to ...

Paula is listening but not really paying attention. In the middle of Yaseen's explanation, she remembers her phone call.

PAULA

Oh yeah, OK, I get it but (one) I've got a call on hold and (two) I'm pretty busy right now and (three) I'm not interested.

She begins to shut the door.

YASEEN

I understand, and I'm sorry to bother you, but I did mention that your boss, James Oberon, said he wants you to handle this? He went to college with the owner of Black Starline and ...

PAULA

(looks hard at Yaseen)

Well, come on in then.

She holds the door open and Yaseen walks in. Paula returns to her call.

PAULA (contd.)

Anton, darling, something came up ... What? Oh stop that, you pervert. Remember, check up on that other car thing I told you about. Later.

Paula hangs up the phone and turns to see that Yaseen is standing in her living room. Yaseen is obviously not impressed with Paula's conversation. Paula notices this and dismisses it with a toss of her weaved hairdo.

PAULA

So ... how is ol' big Jimbo doing?

YASEEN

Jimbo? Oh, James Oberon! He's okay. He did say

that you were a very dedicated woman who would have no problem supporting what we are doing.

She reaches into her bag and pulls out some papers.

PAULA

You know that I haven't spoken to Jimmy in a long time. Did he say if he's still married?

Yaseen looks over at Paula.

YASEEN

I don't know, but I do want you to know that the film presents ways for African-Americans, through contributions, to have a direct impact on alleviating the social and political problems in South Africa and other troubled areas in the world.

PAULA

You know, I did see all of the Tyler Perry movies. I love it when he dresses up as the grandmother. Man, he's a buttnut but funny as hell.

Yaseen gives Paula a "what planet are you from" look and continues.

YASEEN

Another project that we are in preproduction with is a film primer for corporations who are truly interested in assisting us in changing the rules.

Paula hears buzzwords that trigger her mind into third gear.

PAULA

Whoa, whoa, wait a minute. I was responsible for writing many of those so-called rules, and we are making money. They are all major firms and several of them have holdings in South Africa. Now, what do I tell my people? Don't buy that firm because they have interests there? Hell, half the time I use that point to nail their asses to the wall and finish the deal. This is not about politics. It's just business, baby.

Yaseen takes a seat and pulls out a yellow pad. She tries to write but is having some difficulty.

YASEEN

Actually, you're right. It is about the "almighty dollar," but there are two important things about what I do. You see, the words *show business* mean two things: (one) There is *show*, or the creative factor, and (two) There is *business*. Both of them have to work together in order to work. Many people forget that ... besides, life is what happens while you're busy making other plans.

Paula hands Yaseen a large book. Yaseen places it on her lap to help her write things down.

YASEEN

Over a period of five years, a case study showed that the average white-owned business in South Africa earned roughly fifty times more in profit than any black-owned business. The reason being that black business profits are all but nonexistent.

Yaseen rips away a page of her pad and hands it to Paula. As Paula reads the information, Yaseen catches a glimpse of a yearbook for the Marcus Garvey class of 1975 that sits on her lap. Yaseen covers her mouth. Paula sees her do this.

PAULA

What's wrong? It's just my yearbook from my high school.

YASEEN

You graduated in '75?

PAULA

Yeah, from Marcus Garvey, with high honors. In fact, I did win ...

YASEEN

(interrupting)

So did I!

PAULA

You got high honors too?

YASEEN

No, I graduated from Garvey High too, in 1975.

Paula looks at Yaseen's face, trying to remember her.

PAULA

What's your name again?

Yaseen looks at her, confused.

YASEEN

Yaseen Nou—

PAULA
(waving her off)
No, no, no, what's your *real* name?

YASEEN
(slowly)

Janet Moore.

PAULA

Janet Moore ... Janet Moore ... I don't remember a
Moore at all. Did you have any brothers or sisters?

Yaseen shakes her head as she thumbs through the yearbook.

PAULA

Wait a minute! Were you the Moore who was in
my homeroom? The teacher's name was ... Eason.
Miss Eason. I remember that she had a thing for me.

Yaseen doesn't reply, but looks at Paula, remembering.

PAULA

Were you on the prom committee? What about the paper? Did you write for the *Gladiator*?

YASEEN

No, I didn't get into any of that stuff. I kept to myself pretty much ... none of that stuff really interested me.

PAULA

Well, that doesn't matter but it's good to see somebody from home base ... So, how you doin'?

YASEEN

I've been okay for the most part. You, know just taking it a day at a time. You know that life is a series of problems and how you handle them will dictate the quality of your life. What about yourself?

PAULA

I'm doing great. You know, just trying to enjoy myself at any cost.

Paula slowly walks to her kitchen and pulls out a bottle of port wine.

PAULA

My, my, my ... a blast from the past. This calls for the good stuff. It's a 1949 Fonseca and it will knock you out.

Paula waves the bottle in Yaseen's direction.

YASEEN

I never had it, but I'll try anything once.

Paula reenters the living room with two glasses and the port. She fills the glasses to the brim.

PAULA

So, who'd you do time with?

YASEEN

Do time with? Oh, I get it. No, I didn't have many friends and didn't "do time" with anyone.

Paula goes through the yearbook.

PAULA

Man, I can't remember the last time I thought of those days. Cheerleading, the sorority sisters, hanging out. Some of those parties got out of control.

Paula holds up her glass. Yaseen lifts hers and they toast the old days. Paula empties her glass quickly. Yaseen smiles and follows suit.

PAULA

Those were the days. Do you remember ... oh, what was his name? Mr. Jamison, the physics teacher.

YASEEN

Yeah ... tall guy, nice build. I had a crush—

PAULA

(interrupting)

Nice build. Baby, Daddy was a stallion and a half. I remember I blew three tests in a row. He made me stay after class every day for a week. Needless to say, I tried to blow as many tests as possible after that. Know what I'm saying?

As Paula speaks, Yaseen gazes into her wine glass. She takes another sip.

PAULA

How 'bout you? Do you look back at old Garvey with fond memories?

YASEEN

Yeah, some memories stay with us forever ... unfortunately. Have you run into anyone else from Garvey since grad day?

PAULA

No, not really ... Wait a minute, I did run into ... who was it? Judy ... Jane Siegfried or something like that.

Yaseen takes her glass from her mouth quickly.

YASEEN

Yeah, Judy Seaver ... I remember her.

PAULA

Girl, let me tell ya, my girl was fat, barefoot and pregnant ... A love heifer, baby!

Yaseen takes a long, slow sip. Paula drains her drink as she giggles at her own joke. Paula stands up and goes into the kitchen.

PAULA

So tell me, what have you been doing with yourself?

YASEEN

Well, after graduation, I got the hell out of Dodge. I had to ... It felt like the school and the people were trying to strangle me or something.

As Yaseen talks, Paula pulls out another bottle of port and uncorks it on the counter. However, she listens to her guest very closely, almost studying her.

YASEEN

... Anyhow, I left like a shot and joined the Peace Corps. When I landed in Mother Africa, I ... I felt reborn. It was like all the stuff I'd done in the past was just ... history.

Paula comes back into the living room carrying a fresh bottle. She pours some into her glass and then Yaseen's. Out of the blue the phone rings. Paula answers it.

PAULA

(cheerful)

Hello ... hey, girl, what you wearing? Guess what? You'll never guess who's over. Nope, not him either ... Ooh, I haven't seen him in ages ... Listen now, remember Janet Hayes from Garvey? I didn't either, but she went to Garvey. Yeah, Janet ... Yaseen, do you remember Susan James? She was a couple of years ahead of us. You might remember her sister, Pam James. She was the co-captain of the cheerleading squad with me back in the day.

Yaseen is taking little interest in Paula's conversation until Pam James is mentioned. She turns toward Paula with a look of surprise on her face, indicating a bad memory is being dragged to the forefront of her mind.

YASEEN

What did you say?

PAULA

You know Pam James. She was really popular. She died in that accident.

YASEEN

Yeah, I remember her. I remember her very well. I haven't thought of her in ages, though.

PAULA

Yeah, a lot of people don't think about her. Susie, I
gotta run. Listen, I'll see you on the eighth, out on
the island, okay? Take care. Later.

Paula hangs up the phone and leans back on the sofa.

PAULA (contd.)

Where were we? Oh, that's right—Africa! Our so-
called native land. You know, I went to Africa on
business once. It was hot, nasty and smelly. Shit,
give me the Hamptons 24-7-365.

Yaseen stares at her for a moment. Paula sees that Yaseen is
pissed and laughs again.

PAULA

(with a wave of her hand)

Girlfriend, lighten up ... Go on with your story.

YASEEN

Well, Africa was fantastic. I guess I could say that it
saved my life. For the first time I felt relaxed ... like I
didn't have to prove anything to anyone.

PAULA

I took a different route. Being that I was all everything in high school, I could go wherever I wanted
to. Anyhoo, I chose an all-white college because I
wanted a good education and 'cuz I knew how to

party. Well, after four years of undergrad and two years of grad school, I went out into the real world ... and let me tell you something about the "real" world, girl. Most of the people in it go through it dazed and overwhelmed. Not knowing what to do or who to do it to. That bullshit about "a child shall lead them" is just that—bullshit. A woman shall do the *leading*, the *thinking* and the *fucking*.

Paula's head moves back and forth as she finishes her sentence. She throws her head back and laughs. Her laugh is filled with humor and cynicism. Yaseen smiles slyly at her and studies her host.

PAULA (contd.)
Speaking of a good thing, who was workin' you in the old days?

Yaseen takes the glass from her mouth and stares into Paula's eyes. She is caught off-guard by the question.

YASEEN
No one. No one at all. I was kinda shy in those days. Oh, I liked some guys, but they didn't know I was alive ...

PAULA
Do you remember David Sampson, the soccer player? Girl, he was my heart and soul. Me and

David were joined at the you-know-what.

YASEEN

Oh, yeah I do. Didn't he have a brother who was ...

PAULA

Ohhh, yes, his little brother Mark? He was on the soccer team too, or was it football?

YASEEN

Soccer, for two years. He was cute, too. He's gone now, isn't he?

PAULA

I don't know; I was too hot for his brother. He was the captain of the soccer team. Oh, and don't forget Robby. He played, what is that ... oh, forward on the basketball team. I was busy, baby. I guess the question is who *wasn't* I doin'?

YASEEN

I was saying that David and I were friends, and ...

PAULA

Oh, that's right! David! You know, he just came out of nowhere. It was like nobody ever noticed him. Girl, he was young but he was fine! He stared hanging with my crew then.

YASEEN

(softly)

Yeah ... I remember that.

Paula interrupts Yaseen for what seems like the hundredth time. Yaseen is becoming annoyed with the pattern. We can see the strain on her face as Paula interrupts her again.

PAULA

Yes, those were the days. We had a ball, you know. Come to think of it, everybody in my crew was a ...

The lights go dim. A spotlight hits Paula.

PAULA

... a jock or a cheerleader. We were so hot ... We ran that fuckin' school. We did whatever we wanted and we got away with it. We tried to get a hold of the best of everything even back then. Oh, what days ... but it wasn't an everyday party. You had to stay sharp to stay on top. There was always somebody around who thought they were better or knew more than you did.

The spotlight hits Yaseen.

YASEEN

... A jock or a cheerleader. They're all the same, prancing and playing around like they own everything and everyone. And if you weren't part of that clique you were nowhere. A nothing. A faceless and meaningless nothing. They wouldn't even let me in. Every club I tried to join ... They said it was my grades but they acted like they didn't like my looks

or my clothes ... anything. I was just written off! It
... it was like I never existed. All I wanted was to
belong. God, I hated it ... I hated them!

Paula is startled by Yaseen's outburst. Yaseen is visibly upset.

YASEEN
(quietly)
But I showed them ... I showed them all.

Paula reaches out and tenderly touches Yaseen's clenched fist,
which relaxes at the contact.

PAULA
Are you all right?

Yaseen looks up and sees Paula staring at her.

YASEEN
Yeah, I'm okay, thanks.

Paula stands up and walks over to the stereo system.

PAULA
I got something that will bring back some memories.

She turns on her iPod, which is connected to speakers. The

song is "Yin and Yang." Paula half dances, half stumbles back over to the couch and sits down close to Yaseen, who recognizes the song and begins to hum. Paula looks through the yearbook.

PAULA
(sees her picture)
Do you think that I've changed over the past thirty-three years?

YASEEN
(between tokes)
No, not really.

PAULA
Where's your picture?

Paula takes the yearbook and tries to find Yaseen's picture. She turns to the "N's" and cannot find Yaseen.

PAULA
I can't seem to find you.

YASEEN
Try under Janet Moore.

Paula flips to the "M's" and still doesn't see her.

PAULA
I still don't see you, honey.

YASEEN
Oh yeah ... I was busy that day.

PAULA

Oh, I see.

Yaseen leans over to the book and flips through the pages. She points out a picture of a very pretty young lady. Paula slides closer to look at the girl's picture.

YASEEN

I remember her. Karen Nelson—she was okay in my book.

PAULA

Mine too. I had some nice friends. Here's Chris Moses. He was cool. I wonder what he's doing now.

Yaseen shrugs slightly as she flips a couple of pages. She stops and we see a picture of a handsome young man in a tie and jacket. Directly underneath the photo we see another photo of a young man with a star underneath his name. The number 4 is written under his name. His name is Duane Holmes.

PAULA

Hey, I remember him. He stayed clean all the time. That tie and jacket stayed on him even if it was a hundred degrees.

Yaseen laughs.

YASEEN

And remember that little briefcase he used to carry?
Now, what do you think he had in that briefcase?

They both laugh.

PAULA/YASEEN

A spare suit!

By this point both woman are very intoxicated. Two bottles of
wine and the weed have taken effect. Yaseen and Paula fall over
each other, laughing hysterically. The beginning of something
special can be felt. Yaseen glances down at the yearbook and
stops laughing as she looks more closely at the picture of Duane
Holmes. She sees the star, and the number 4 written there.
Paula recovers from laughing as she sees Yaseen's expression
change. She looks down at the book.

PAULA

What a piece of work.

Yaseen, deep in thought, doesn't reply. She mutters a name under her breath and continues to flip through the yearbook.

YASEEN

Karen Nelson ...

Yaseen turns to the pages to a photo of a young woman, Karen

Nelson. There is a star with a #1 inside it. The humor slowly drops from Paula's face as she watches Yaseen go through the book.

PAULA
(remembering)

It's strange, they just started dying one year and nobody knew why ... had to be horrible accidents. I decided to put stars by their names so I'd never forget them. By the time we graduated seven of them were gone. Some of them died hard ... Paula's voice trails off. She reaches over and takes the yearbook from Yaseen. Placing it on her lap she turns to find the second of her unfortunate friends. Paula goes to the rear of the book and stops.

PAULA (contd.)

She was the second one that—

Paula begins to move closer to Yaseen to show her the picture, but before she can speak Yaseen says something.

YASEEN
(softly)

Pam James ...

Paula stares at Yaseen. She looks down at the photo. We see the photo and the star with a #2 inside it. Paula looks up at Yaseen, surprised. She begins to flip back through the yearbook.

YASEEN (contd.)

Duane Holmes ...

Paula stops at Duane's picture. We see a #3 with a star around it. Paula looks up from the yearbook at Yaseen. Yaseen stares straight at her. Paula turns one more page, never taking her eyes off of Yaseen. Yaseen sits back. Several moments pass. Yaseen stares at Paula coolly. Her gaze doesn't break. Paula's expression changes to one of an inner calm. She understands. Not only does Yaseen know who was killed; more important, she knows what order they died in. The explanation is obvious. A competitor. Paula smiles. She opens the book and turns the pages. Paula stops midway through the book and looks straight at Yaseen, placing the yearbook on the couch between them.

PAULA

It was you ... Susan Charlotte, the teacher couldn't get her off the parallel bars. She was wrapped around it by her neck. You know, it was sort of her fault. The first thing we learned was to check out her equipment. Never start a workout doing a safety check. I heard that her skin was the only thing holding her head on. See, she thought she was so hot, she thought she was the best thing and so did some of the others ... but if she was, how come she didn't know the bar was loose?

Paula's voice trails off as she continues to flip through more pages. She talks in a slow whisper. Yaseen watches the pages turn and Paula's face.

PAULA

Rob Law ... you know, the stallion's son. Now he was smart and stuff. You probably remember, he was up for class valedictorian the same year I was. He was always in the lab mixing chemicals up, writing formulas, talking with the teacher. You'd think he'd know enough to read the labels—any fool knows that when you mix potassium and acid 619 together it results in an explosion. It sticks to you and burns ... he should've known that. Even *I* know that. Shit, the buttnut used to think he was smarter than me. They were scraping Robby off the walls for weeks.

Paula looks down at his picture, smiles slightly and makes a sound like an explosion. Yaseen watches her.

PAULA (contd.)

Missy Jones. She was my best friend. I told that girl everything. I didn't have a whole lot of real friends ... really couldn't afford to. I remember when I first told her about Jimmy and that I thought I was in love with him. We all started hangin' out. After a while they started hanging without me ... They didn't think I knew, but I did all right. On the way home, I caved in her skull with a hammer.

She quickly puts out her cig with a strong move.

                    YASEEN

Hmm ... Death is something we all have in common.

                    PAULA

I don't know why I'm telling you this. You see, I'm the best. I did what I had to do and I'd do it again in a fuckin' heartbeat.

Yaseen grins slyly, not at all surprised at what Paula has just told her. She stands and stretches.

                    YASEEN

Must've been a drag trying to think of new ways to eliminate your competition. Loosened parallel bars? Explosions? I'm impressed, but I never went to so much trouble. All I did was get rid of the ones who caused the most problems for me. They didn't know what hit them when I killed them.

Paula looks at Yaseen in a different light.

                    PAULA

You're impressed?

YASEEN

Oh, you're so creative ... I mean, it's much more than I'd expect from a pompom girl. But this head-smashing business ... pretty unimaginative. I found out that poison did the job and left no evidence. Guess it was really messing with you, huh?

Paula's mouth snaps open and she's prepared to deliver a stinging reply, but then she recognizes the ploy and simply relaxes.

YASEEN (contd.)

You know, you asked me if I thought you'd changed. I know what I said before, but I think you have. You're older and a little smarter, but it sort of seems that the stupid attitude you had in high school has grown up with you and just taken you over completely. Too bad ... you had a chance to ...

Paula jumps up.

PAULA

A *chance*? Listen up, girlfriend. High school taught me how to get rid of the competition in my life. That's what school is all about, right?

Yaseen smiles.

YASEEN

Hey, I suppose it is.

Pause. Paula smiles.

YASEEN (contd.)

What it isn't, though, is people like you running over the less ambitious. You and your herd of whores did more damage than you will ever know. There were plenty of us who wanted to be in the main clique but we didn't match up to your qualities.

PAULA

Those who can't keep up, don't. Their or you are just wasting space.

YASEEN

I get it now. People who are beneath you die and those above you die too with no regret or emotion. Good plan.

PAULA

(trying to stay cool)

You've got some nerve ...

YASEEN

No, not some nerve but a lot of time invested. I spent almost half my life trying to adjust to the shit your type put me though. That's a hard, full-time job, and very, very painful. I could only stand so much. The pressure was unbelievable so I did what I had to do. Payback is a bitch ...

PAULA

(interrupting)

Listen, you don't have to—

YASEEN

(cutting her off)

Shut up! I was busy trying to get through the day and adjust to what I thought you people wanted. Then one day it dawned on me. I won't adjust myself. I'll adjust you! It worked and I liked it. Each time I did it, it made me stronger and better. Better than them ... and better than you.

She turns to look hard at Paula.

PAULA

You're one sick bitch.

YASEEN

Yeah, maybe I was, but not anymore, girlfriend.

PAULA

(sarcastically)

Oh really?

YASEEN

(seductively)

Really. You know, back then I never imagined there was someone else out there like me, but there was ...

PAULA

Wrong, homegirl. I'm not like you at all. I'm the best at whatever I do. The best. I'm one of a kind ... Don't forget that.

Paula turns away from Yaseen.

YASEEN

You may think you're the best, but I'll always be better than you in everything.

Yaseen turns her back to Paula. Then, in a split second, both women turn toward each other in a rush and attack.

BLACK.

Chapter 17
A Random Dream Thought ...

TODAY

He awoke with a start, but knowing that he was not too late to start his busy morning. His alarm clock never failed him. It was the latest in technology.

He knew that his life was good, better than his father's and his grandfather's. He didn't know how it could get any better. He had the best of everything. No, he wasn't a rich man but he could afford the best for his family because he worked hard and it had paid off in spades.

He jumped out of bed and quickly got dressed, knowing what the day had in store for him. His mind was filled with the talk of something new that would change life as he knew it. At first he thought it was the grog talking, but something about it niggled. You see, it was a stranger from the hinterlands who came in talking of tales that were foreign to him and his kind. Many of his kindred laughed it off as drunken talk, but it stuck with him till the morning. Maybe it was the way the stranger was dressed or his manner of speech or even the strange symbols he wrote on the top of the bar.

"Times are a-changing, my good friends," he said, laughing

at them.

"But why? We have everything we need," Balter answered.

"Are you sure of that?" he asked slyly.

The men looked at each other as if they had been asked a riddle they didn't know the answer to.

"Let me ask you one simple question: Are you free people?" He waited for an answer.

The men shuffled their feet, looking down.

"I work my own land!" he answered heatedly.

"Ah, is that so? Do you keep all the profits from your work?"

"Ah, well no, but I do get ..."

"How many years are you indebted to your master?" He raised an eyebrow.

He looked down, embarrassed by his question, even though many of my friends were in the same situation.

"Ten, maybe twenty years. Why do you ask?" He tried to put up a brave front.

Balter put a hand on his shoulder, rubbing it. "It's nothing to be afraid of, my friend. Your children's lives will much better—they will be free. Plus, there is something else ..."

That was when he wrote some symbols on the top of the bar: CARPE DIEM.

We all stared at the symbols in awe, not knowing what he had written, but knowing it was important.

"Seize the day," he said with reverence.

We repeated what he said in a hushed whisper.

He went on to tell us about a man in a land called Germany

who had invented something called the printing press, and how this invention had started something called the Renaissance.

Things would never be the same.

He came out of his daydream beside his baby girl and boy, who were dressed in rags. He pulled on his shirt. He decided then and there to make a true difference in their lives. He went to the fireplace and got a piece of charcoal and closed his eyes, trying to remember what the man wrote. Slowly he wrote down what he had, letter for letter: CARPE DIEM.

He picked up his children, cradling them closely.

"Seize the day ... *seize the day!*" he told them.

Chapter 18

MASTER OF TIME AND SPACE

INTRODUCTION

I was writing project after project, when I had an idea based on a Rod Serling story. In his story a man creates a huge robot that will destroy all of humanity. It will be self-automated and the man will be locked inside so no one will be able to get inside it. At the last moment he gets inside the robot and locks himself in, but realizes he doesn't have the key to start the thing up.

I liked the Serling story and wanted to write something with the same theme. Many of my ideas come from *The Twilight Zone*. It is a show that allows your mind to wander from place to place. I suspect that it is based on Dream Thinking.

My idea came to me one day, so I started to write it. I chose to base it on being in high school and being bullied. I wasn't bullied in school, but I knew people who were. I didn't like it, but it was one of the things that went on. I asked myself the "What if?" question, and it came to me.

This is the first story I wrote that has some sexual undertones. They are not graphic, but they do seem to work within the story.

MASTER OF TIME AND SPACE

For years, Jonas T. Samuels had carefully planned and prepared for this moment. He was about to claim his place in the Destiny of Humankind. He was the Master of Time and Space, and it was time for the world to know it.

They would shake with fear from what he was about to do to them. The people (and he had a list) who had screwed him over or laughed at him over the years would pay for their insolence. The true joke was that they wouldn't even know it. Only he would process this knowledge, giving him an even greater sense of power.

He smiled, and felt a warm and comforting feeling slide over his body. He masturbated to an extreme orgasm, readying himself for the task at hand.

Coming out of the shower, he looked down at his uniform and equipment. It had taken years to design and millions of dollars to pay for, but it was worth it. It wasn't just the latest in technology; it was way ahead of the curve in so many ways. To keep it a secret, he had selected different companies to build the various elements, and none knew what the others were building. No one was even close to understanding the concepts utilized in inventing his baby. He held up a gothic novel of his favorite superhero, looking at himself in a mirror.

He was so close.

He sat down and oiled up his body, preparing it for the suit, and remembered how it all began.

2005

In high school he got his ass kicked every other day for several years. They would take turns and make bets on how fast they could get Jonas to pee in his pants. Yes, it was embarrassing but there was nothing he could do about it. He told his parents, teachers and friends but no one could do anything to make it stop. He resigned himself to it, and even scheduled it into his daily life.

It was a Wednesday, October 13 to be exact, when something changed. Jimmy Herr, the baddest of the bad, had decided it was his turn to have some fun. He had cornered Jonas in the shower and dragged him out into the gym when the coach was not there. The entire girls' ninth grade was there to see him. When he saw Jimmy's fist pull back to hit him in the face, he closed his eyes.

But nothing happened.

He slowly opened an eye to see that everyone was frozen, not moving a muscle. Jimmy's fist was an inch away from his nose. He stepped around it and looked around, taking in the bizarre scene. He walked around the watching crowd, seeing how they were in mid-cheer as he was about to get his face remodeled.

Tammy Hinman, captain of the cheerleaders, was in mid-jump. Her skirt was over her waist, showing off a pair of white cotton panties. Jonas looked around the gym, and then touched her down there. That's when everything came back to life. Jimmy's fist hit the wall and broke in a dozen places. Everyone screamed. In the chaos, and before they saw him, he ran away. From that day forward, no one messed with him again. Even Tammy smiled at him in the hallways.

As hard as he tried, he couldn't make it happen again. He read everything he could on time travel and teleportation, but nothing applied to what had happened to him. He knew something had happened but he didn't know what.

2010

After graduation, he went to college and studied physics and thermal dynamics, almost getting his PhD. However, no one was willing to listen to his experience-based theories about time and space. They just laughed. Even Stephen Hawking's theories didn't hold a candle to what he had learned.

Before long, he had to take a job at Burger King to survive. He kept up his research, expanding it to reading science fiction and gothic novels. He became fascinated with superheroes and really wanted to be one.

One day, while coming out of the Forbidden Planet on Broadway in New York City, he was crossing the street, reading the latest *Next Men* gothic novel, when he heard a noise and looked up. A truck was about to slam into him, head on. He closed his eyes.

Nothing happened.

He slowly opened his eyes, and then started to laugh. It had happened again. That was when he understood what had transpired. During a time of possible death he had the ability to stop time and space. He walked out of the path of the oncoming truck and wondered how to start it up again. Then he saw a girl frozen in mid-step across the street. Without thinking, he reached over and squeezed her right breast. It was like turning on the power. Everything started up again. She looked at him with surprise in her eyes. He smiled and kept on walking. He now knew the secret ... the secret of becoming the master of time and space.

Later that year, he was in a bank thinking about how to use his newfound power when he heard several gunshots fired. He turned to see several robbers in mid-heist. He started to run, but stopped when he heard another gunshot. He closed his eyes, terrified of what might happen.

Then he remembered and laughed. Slowly, he turned and saw a shotgun bullet inches from his face, frozen in mid-air. He walked around it and surveyed the situation. That's when it caught his eye.

The money.

Without a care in the world, he strolled over and grabbed it, and started whistling as he exited. Once he was out of the bank, he rubbed a woman's ass, turning it all back on.

Later that day, he read that they had captured the thieves. The thing that really caught his attention was the talk of a man disappearing from sight with the money.

2020

Over the next ten years he prepared himself physically and technically for what was to happen. Once a year he was lucky enough to use his gift to secure funds from banking institutions to finance his goals. He discovered that the more intense the danger of his possible death the longer the effect lasted. Even though he had the ability to shut it down by making sexual contact, there had been times when he let it last and discovered that over time the effect slowly wore off and time caught up with him. This was an important discovery and he incorporated it into the grand plan of his destiny.

2030

Today was the day. He had spent almost a million dollars to design and complete his MTSS (Master/Time/Space/Suit). In it was everything he would need to complete his mission. His research showed that if the element of danger was extremely high, he could not only stop time, but reverse it. His plan was to commit suicide by jumping off a building. That way he could reverse time to a point where he could change things in society to make it better for the little guy—people like him, who deserved a second chance and a better lot in life.

He put on his skintight suit. He was now a superhero. It felt right. Wearing an overcoat, he walked out into society as if for the last time, knowing that it was about to change forever.

He smiled.

He got a tourist ticket to the top of the Empire State Building. On the observation deck, he slowly climbed out over the fencing, looking out at his true destiny. Then he leaped out, performing a perfect swan dive. Oh yeah, he looked good.

But something was different this time.

He was not stopping. He closed his eyes and opened them again, but he was still falling. Time was continuing. What was the problem? Then it hit him, square in the face. Each time in the past when it had happened he had been in danger of death, but not by his hand; by the hands of others. Even the bank jobs had been at the hands of other robbers, and he had stopped their movement.

This was not good ...

Chapter 19
A Final Random Dream Thought ...

A FINAL WORD
FROM OUR SPONSOR

Due to a series of international incidents the powers that be have engineered the end of the world. The president has decided to contact the top advertising company in the country and ask it to come up with a commercial that would thank the people of America for their help. The company assembles its best and brightest to design the commercial. They argue over what they should say and how to say to say it. The younger executives think the spot should be aimed at the MTV generation while the more conservative members of the team believe that substance will get the job done. They are deadlocked; neither side will give in. Desperate to reach a decision, they decide to try their ideas out on the pizza-delivery guy. He watches the spec spots that each team has put together. Neither one of them has any effect on him. He finally tells them that the best approach is the simplest one. The evening of the attack, the commercial airs on every network save for one independent station that decided to stay with its scheduled programming.

UPDATE

I want to bring you up to date on what's going on in my life. First, I'm having some health problems. I am on dialysis three days a week. I have had to go into the hospital several times over the years. I am seeing many doctors that are helping me.

In 2009 I moved back to my hometown of Rochester, NY. I quit my job at Fox TV because I was having seizures and bouts of pancreatitis. I had gone into rehab several times to get better (it did finally work). Being home changed my life in many ways. I began seeing new doctors who are helping me stay well. Like I said in my introduction: "Life is what happens while you're making other plans."

However, I have been busy making plans. I formed a film-production organization that is busy producing books, films and radio plays. Speaking of radio plays: I am busy turning *Dream Think* into a series of radio dramas for commercial radio and my own personal podcast.

I have looked back into my library of scripts and stories and decided to try and push them into being produced as feature films and books. One thing that has changed in the last several years is the development of more and more outlets for ideas or dreams. I plan to use them to produce projects.

I believe that my book will either be a book of one of my screenplays or an autobiography (which I plan to call *Forrest*

Hump).

The last thing I want to do is to give you YouTube channel link to check out some of my work: https://www.youtube.com/channel/uchgievrgzpv69_tdghwtt1a. Please watch the videos and subscribe to my channel.

Thank you for reading this book, and I wish you good and productive Dream Thinking.

—DCT

ABOUT THE AUTHOR

David C. Taylor was born and raised in Henrietta, NY. He graduated from Howard University in 1982 with a degree in film and television production. His feature-film experience includes working on *She's Gotta Have It* (PA), *School Daze* (2nd AD), *Girl 6* (video TD), *Summer of Sam* (additional sound and video recordist), and *Dead Presidents* (writer, director, editor, behind the scenes/EPK). The short film *The Session*, which won the Paul Robeson Award and the Black Filmmakers Foundation Award, was based on his skit "The Deprogrammer." It was subsequently produced as a feature film by Spike Lee in 1994.

Visit his YouTube channel at www.youtube.com/channel/UChgieVrGzPV69_tDGHWTT1A, and his blog at davidctaylor147.wordpress.com. For more reviews and comments, please visit www.dreamthinkbook.com.